DON'T DO THIS AT HOME
(When growing up had few limits)

By
Peter H Rees

Published by New Generation Publishing in 2022

Copyright © Peter H Rees 2022

First Edition

ISBN   978-1-80369275-3

www.newgeneration-publishing.com

New Generation Publishing

CONTENTS

INTRODUCTION

To begin at the beginning. I was born in 1949 which, as I write these words, makes me seventy – three years of age. I have always argued that people of my generation had the best of times. That, of course, is my opinion and many, I'm sure, would disagree. When I was a teenager jobs were plentiful. The words "unemployment" and "redundancy" were almost unknown and when leaving school I never worried as to whether or not I would find a job. My main concern was 'which' job, of the many on offer, I wanted. I was offered three apprenticeships, not because of any innate brilliance but rather because that was the way things were.

There were no personal computers or 'I' phones and social media consisted of people talking to each other, writing letters or using up pennies in the all-important red telephone box that each village had. Tertiary education was free, the family GP would see you at home and would sometimes call in unannounced if someone in the family had recently been ill. There were no supermarkets and villages were full of shops...and pubs! Police officers walked the beat and every village had its own police station and incumbent 'Police Man' who knew which characters he needed to keep an eye on. Cars were rare and my mates and I played care free in the streets. There was true community spirit with unlocked doors and twitching curtains.

I, like most of my peers, made my own fun out and about and I only really went into my bedroom to sleep. On a weekend, free from school, I would be out for hours exploring far and wide and only return home when it was tea time. It is, in the main, these times that the stories in this book are all about...making my own fun and often getting up to innocent mischief. The stories are not in any form of chronological order and one can dip into them as and how you wish. I hope you enjoy.

Many of the names of characters in my stories I have changed to protect the innocent...as well as the guilty! I have also used Imperial measurements as I just 'can't be asked' to convert them into Metric so there! I was a child of the 1950's and 1960'a after all. In my mind's eye I can picture a gallon of petrol, but not a litre.

I wish to thank Mr. A.B. Wyze for granting me permission to use extracts from his poem "Tanners and Bobs" which can be found in his book "Back in the Days of Tanners and Bobs" and available from Amazon.

WHERE I GREW UP... MY HOME!

Most of the stories in my collection are about events which occurred in and around my home area in South Wales. As such, I thought it would be useful if I give you some idea of this area in order to help you picture the various places in your mind's eye as you read through the stories. I have not described every street and every building but, instead, have concentrated on the areas and features of the local landscape which are relevant to the following tales. It is hard though to know where to begin.

I suppose it could be argued that both Brian, my brother and myself were lucky to be born and brought up on the Gower Peninsula which is tucked away in South West Wales. In 1956 Gower was the first area in the United Kingdom to be designated an Area Of Outstanding Natural Beauty and deservedly so in my opinion. Nineteen miles long, the peninsula projects westwards into the Bristol Channel and has a wide diversity in geography, history, plants and wildlife.

Its southern coast is dominated by high, rugged limestone cliffs interspaced with sandy beaches, secretive coves and rocky shores. These cliffs were heavily quarried for limestone which was burnt in coal and wood fired lime kilns. The resulting lime powder was used as a fertiliser, for whitewashing houses and was exported elsewhere. Several of these defunct kilns can still be seen dotted around the landscape and, as a boy, some of my mates and myself would sometimes camp out overnight in one or two of the larger ones.

Moving inland from these cliffs, one enters rich agricultural land and pockets of woodland before gently rising onto a long red sandstone ridge which protrudes from the surrounding limestone. Known as Cefn Bryn, the ridge rises to a height of 617 feet. Locals refer to it as the

"Backbone of Gower" as it runs east to west along the length of the peninsula.

The ridge drops away to the north towards a coastline which is a complete contrast to its southern neighbour. Again, the ridge drops down onto agricultural land which, in turn, drops onto saltmarsh which forms the southern edge of the tidal Burry Estuary. As such, compared to Gower's south coast there are few cliffs on this coastline, though there is evidence of quarrying at several locations where the limestone breaks through the landscape.

The village that Brian and I grew up in is known as Penclawdd and sits snuggly, low down on the water's edge on Gower's northern coastline. It is a lovely, ugly village and like many villages in South Wales, its existence is due to coal mining of which much evidence still exists in the form of overgrown spoil heaps and other decaying remnants of industry.

*****

A railway line ran through the village of Penclawdd. At least there *was* a railway line until Doctor Beeching had his way back in the 1960's. Following his big shake up of the railway system throughout the country our village railway line, like many others, vanished; destined to become in later decades, cycle paths, footpaths, bridleways or simply left to rot. The railway that ran through our village had been built back in the 1860's in order to service this pocket of industrial activity. The village had its own docks and, apart from its coal mining heritage, it was renowned for its extensive tinplate, copper and brass works.

*****

Our paternal grandparents lived in a village called Llanmorlais which is about two miles west of Penclawdd where we were both brought up. Llanmorlais, by the way, was the termination point of the railway line which features in several of my stories. The pair of buffers which marked the end of the line were only about a hundred yards past my grandparents' house. When the railway was closed and torn up, the resulting empty area became an extension to our adventure playground with steep, bracken covered earth banks leading down to where the double line of tracks once ran.

The railway replaced the canal as the main transport link until the current road leading into and through the village was built in the 1920's. My parents and grandparents always referred to this highway as *The New Road*. From my point of view though, the road had always been there.

The railway through the village was spanned by four bridges. I say *was* because following the events in my story *Burning One's Bridges*, there were soon only three. Three of the bridges were works of art; built of quality dressed stone and aesthetically pleasing with their neat, artistic corner turrets. They were a testimony to the great skill, care and pride that went into their design and building. It is a pity that only one of them still exists, though one cannot really call it a bridge any more as the railway line that once ran beneath it has been long filled in. Although it still carries road traffic, it now sits on top of many feet and tons of earth.

The bridge concerned with *Burning One's Bridges* was the ugly duckling of the four. Apart from the two stone-built support walls which held back the steep earth banks, the entire edifice was built of wood with an earth covered roadway forming its span. It had no safety rails flanking it at all. As a young boy, I never wondered why this bridge was so very different in design from the other three. Considering its generous width and the complete absence of steps at either end, made me conclude later in life that it was probably built to accommodate the horse and donkey drawn cockle carts that were a common sight in the village back when I was a boy. I may be completely wrong on this point of course. but it seems a reasonable explanation as to why the bridge existed. The bridge would probably have supported a motor vehicle but I never saw one attempt to cross it. The road tracks leading to the bridge were very rough and poor. Good enough for a horse drawn cart but which, I am sure, would have been totally unsuitable for any motorist to venture along.

*****

The village of Penclawdd overlooks vast reaches of tidal salt marsh. Theses marshes form the upper reaches of the Bury Estuary which flows out into Carmarthen Bay and the Bristol Channel beyond. They are characterised by raised mud banks; topped with flat green carpets of salt resistant turf and spiky spartina cordgrass. Such flora supports a wealth of marine and bird life and at low tides sheep and horses graze the lush grass.

Allegedly, the horses are the descendants of those that pulled the cockle carts that were once a common sight in the village. They are born, live and die on the marshes and are often seen at high tides standing rock solid still, surrounded by water. I have witnessed horses standing there with water up to their necks and once saw a foal standing on its mother's back whilst they both waited patiently for the waters to recede. During the summer months this unusual display in equine behaviour is quite the tourist attraction. The sheep, however, are put out to graze on the marshes deliberately and are the source of the famed Gower Salt Marsh Lamb which is sold locally and elsewhere.

Geographically, *The Marsh* as it is known locally, runs east/west with its north and south edges guarded by two tidal rivers. These rivers make access difficult, which usually involves wading through slimy mud and fast flowing tidal water. Adding to these problems, the whole area is punctuated by long meandering rivers which have been carved out of the mud by the ebb and flow of timeless tides. These are known as *pills* which vary dramatically in terms of length, width and depth. These really are a maze and unless one is familiar with the area, they can really hinder the progress of the duck shooter or fisherman and the like.

On an incoming high tide and once the rivers and pills are filled to their tops, the water spills over the banks and travels over the flat terrain faster than one can walk. It can be a dangerous place to be and, over the years, there have been several occasions when cockle gatherers and others were caught out by this fast tide and paid the ultimate price for doing so. Fog and mists are another hazard as one can easily lose one's sense of direction. I was once told that if I was ever caught out on the marshes by fog or mist, then a trick to find safety would be to follow the sheep tracks in the grass. These might lead me on a roundabout route, but would eventually get me ashore safely. Fortunately, neither my brother of myself ever had to use this trick.

It is such hazards that make life somewhat difficult for anyone wanting to venture out onto the marshes. One has to keep an eye on the tides and the amount of water running in the tidal river that parallels the shoreline of the village. My brother and his mates from the shooting fraternity were no strangers to the need to carefully scrutinise the tides, as evidenced in my story *Time And Tide Wait For No Man.*

*****

For the first five years of my life we, as a family, lived with my maternal grandfather and his other daughter, my aunt. The house sat right at the edge of the estuary with only the main road and a wide grass verge separating its front boundary from the sea wall. Its design was typical for the time, both for the village where I lived and for South Wales as a whole.

To explain the function of each downstairs room I want you to imagine that you are a visitor. At the very back of the house there was a kitchen, usually small and with a lean-to roof. You would never go in there unless you were either a family member or very well known to the household. As a visitor you would normally be restricted to the living room.

This was the heart of the house where you would sit and gossip and politely sip your tea which you would certainly be offered…in a cup and saucer of course. There were no mugs in those days.

If lucky, you might also be offered a Welsh cake or two or a slice of apple or blackberry tart, all home made and probably still warm from the oven. In this room the household ate its meals, watched television (One channel only and that was in black and white), read the newspapers, did one's homework, played and just generally lived. It was always warm and cosy. It was home.

Moving forward through the house next came the middle room. Again, depending how well you were known, you might be escorted into its comfortable space to be shown a new piece of furniture or new curtains and such. Normally, no one ever sat down in there even though it had the grandest of chairs. Then, in the very front of the house came the eponymously named front room. This was hallowed ground which contained the piano and other musical instruments. Only if you were a very special visitor, akin to the Queen of England, would you be allowed in there. It was my grandfather's inner sanctum where he read his books, played the piano, played the cello and violin though not at the same time!

The room had a huge and ornate mirror over the fireplace, the reflection of which made the room seem even bigger. In fact, the word 'room' was considered an inadequate word to describe this space and hence it was known as the front *parlour*. To my young nose it even smelt differently to the other rooms. Of tobacco pipe smoke, polish, cleanliness and *very* grand.

*****

During the times when I was a lad it was usual for each village to have its own police station with incumbent police officer. The *village policeman* as he was known, lived at the police station. As well as being his home the station was his base, complete with cells for those who fell on the wrong side of the law. Our village of Penclawdd was no exception. The substantial red bricked building with its blue lamp had its own air of authority and when in its vicinity, I would be on my best behaviour. When I was naughty, my mother often threatened to take me there and have me locked up… the thought of which soon put me back on the straight and narrow.

She did actually once carry out her threat. In probable collusion with the police officer, she told him of my bad behaviour of which he was no doubt thoroughly and visibly shocked about. After showing me the foreboding and echoing cells, complete with green and white glazed tiles, he let me off with a warning. The building is still there but has long since been turned into domestic accommodation… flats I believe.

Our village policeman was Police Constable Davies or Mr. Davies as we called him. If you read my story *Discipline Ain't What It Used To Be,* then you will learn of his interpretation of law and punishment. To me as a lad, he was a giant of a man… at least 6' 13" tall… who kept his wary eye on the whole village. Being a permanent member of the community he soon got to know who the local rotten apples were and where, if he needed to, find them. He patrolled the village on foot but would sometimes be seen on his sturdy black bicycle. He demanded total respect from us youngsters and he usually got it. If I saw him walking towards me and there was no route of escape, I straightened up, looked smart and greeted him politely.

*****

High up at the top end of my home village of Penclawdd was what one could have called back then, the municipal rubbish tip… the forerunner of the modern recycling centre. To us locals, it was simply known as *The Dump.* The dump was located on the site of a long-abandoned coal mine and was a popular playground to many of us adventurous lads.

Here, the dust carts as we called them, would deposit all the rubbish they had collected from neighbouring households and businesses alike. I am writing here of a time before the concepts of *recycling* and *saving the planet* had even been thought of. There were no black rubbish bags, nor were there any blue, green or pink ones either. All we had back then was the metal rubbish bin into which everything went and which was emptied by the council once every week... Yes. That's right...*every* week!

These were the days before central heating and combi boilers. Houses had coal fires which had to be cleaned out every morning and re-laid with scrunched up newspaper, sticks and coal. I was often given the privilege to light the fire with a single match. I would set light to a corner or edge of newspaper and delight in watching the flames work their way upwards, setting alight the sticks which supported the coal. Soon a steady fire would be burning and kept going throughout the day with the occasional addition of more coal. The old ashes from the previous day's fires, usually still warm, were placed in the metal dust bin ready for the weekly collection.

Anything that could not be fitted into the bin you took to the dump yourself. As such, this vast area contained an eclectic mix of rubbish. There were abandoned motor vehicles, bicycles, furniture, prams, toys, ovens, televisions, fridges, electrical goods of all descriptions, all lying there amongst thousands of bottles, tins, cans, cardboard boxes and goodness knows what. It was quite an adventure going there as one could never tell what one would find. Today though there is no sign of the dump. It was largely levelled and landscaped and is now quite a nice area to walk in.

*****

Penclawdd was, and still is, famous for its cockle industry. These shellfish are collected from the Burry Estuary which flanks the northern shore of the Gower peninsula. I remember very well going out onto the sands with my mother and other relatives to collect a bucket or two of these cockles. They made an excellent supper. The horse and donkey carts are long gone now and have been replaced by land rovers and tractors. At the time of writing, two modern factories in the village are all that remain of the industry which, back in the day, was contributed to by many families. Most of the produce these days leaves the factories in refrigerated lorries to be sold both domestically and in Europe.

Did you know...

Gower is steeped in history and it has more than its fair share of castles and archaeological sites. Probably the most significant and famous site is that known as Paviland Cave which is situated between the villages of Port Eynon and Rhossili. It is where the "Red Lady of Paviland" was found. This is a partial skeleton of a male dyed in red ochre and buried some 33,000 years ago. It is known as the "Red Lady" as the remains were first thought to be of a female from the Roman era. The proper name for this cave is Goat's Hole which was investigated in 1823 when the skeleton was found. The archaeologist was William Buckland, Professor of Geology from Oxford university where, I believe, the original skeleton is kept. Copies of the bones were made and the last time I looked, these were on display in Swansea museum along with other artifacts found on the dig. I read somewhere that the skeleton of the "Red Lady" was the first human fossil to have been found anywhere in the world.

By the way. For those of you who might not know the area, I warn you now that Paviland Cave is very difficult and dangerous to access. Reaching it involves either jumping across a very deep and considerably wide rock chasm or traversing a near vertical cliff face. Whichever way one gets there one needs a head for heights. Its original inhabitants would have had no such difficulty. Way back then, tens of thousands of years ago, the Bristol Channel which now laps at the foot of the cave did not exist. The cave inhabitants would have looked out across a vast wooded plain with exotic animals roaming about. Fossilized trees have been found further up the Bristol Channel coast and during Buckland's dig in 1823, tusks belonging to long dead mammoths were found in the cave.

*****

The railway line through Penclawdd replaced the canal as the main transport link until the current road leading into and through the village was built in the 1920's. The line originated in Swansea and eventually terminated at the village of Llanmorlais about two miles further west of Penclawdd. Llanmorlais was where our paternal grandparents lived. Long before I popped out into this world, the line boasted a passenger service which my parents and grandparents remembered well. From what I have read, the passenger service was terminated in 1931. I remember talking to my maternal grandfather about the days of the railway. He mentioned a chap who lived in Penclawdd who became a bit of local celebrity. His exalted status came about because he had gone all the way to London and back home on the trains... unheard of! To many, this adventure must have been akin to the modern day moon landings?

*****

Going out onto the marshes of The Burry Estuary requires a combination of planning, local knowledge and common sense. The Bristol Channel has the second highest rise and fall of tidal waters in the world, and this affects the speed of water as it enters and leaves the estuary. If you are wondering, *the* world's highest rise and fall of tide occurs in Canada at the Bay of Fundy which separates New Brunswick from Nova Scotia.

TANNERS AND BOBS

By
A.B. WYZE

Back in the days of tanners and bobs
when mothers had patience and fathers had jobs.
When football team families wore hand me down shoes
and TV gave only two channels to choose.

Back in the days of three-penny bits
when schools employed nurses to search for your nits.
When snowballs were harmless and ice slides permitted
and all of your jumpers were warm and hand knitted.

Back in the days of National Health glasses
when teachers all stood at the front of their classes.
When woodwork and pottery were taught in schools
and everyone dreamed of a win on the pools.

Back in the days of Beatles and Stones
when everyone chatted and no-one owned phones.
When children respected what older folks said
and pot was something you kept under the bed.

Back in the days of marbles and jacks
conkers on laces and gaberdine macs.
When chips were all wrapped up in yesterday's news
and skiffle grew up into rhythm and blues.

Back in the days of pennies for guys
when only one person wore Santa's disguise.
When Meccano was the latest big craze
and Christmas lasted no more than twelve days.

Back in the days when school milk was free
when families sat at the table for tea.
When winter was winter all knee deep in snow
and down at the Co-op your divvy would grow.

Back in the days when I was a lad
I can't help smile at the fun that I had.
With hopscotch and roller skates and snowballs to lob
all back in the days of tanners and bobs.

DISCIPLINE AIN'T WHAT IT USED TO BE

I was very fortunate during my school years in the sense that all three schools attended, infants, primary and secondary were all within walking distance from home. These were the days when one usually walked everywhere. There was no such thing as the 'school run' and anyone not wanting to catch a bus, walked to school. Living so close also meant that I could, on most school days, get home for dinner and not have to suffer the creamy mashed potatoes and rice and jam desert of school fare…ugh!

My primary school was of a design very common way back then. A stone built, solid building, which made us pupils sense its authority as soon as we entered the gates. The school even had its own particular smell which gently wafted its way throughout the entire building. It was, as I remember, a cocktail of fine chalk dust, leather from our school satchels, wood polish, disinfectant and laced with the ever-present background aroma of school dinners. On wet days the musty, dank smell of drying coats which hung in obedient rows in the lobbies could be added to the cocktail.

The windows were tall, narrow and stretched upwards towards the sky. The classrooms themselves were big and dominating to our young eyes. The windows were so high that to open or close them, the teacher had to use a very long wooden pole with a metal hook on its business end. Sometimes a pupil would be chosen to perform this important task. To be thus selected was considered a great honour. I always felt so important when I, myself, was tasked with this job. With muscles tensed, and tongue extended between my lips in pure concentration, I would raise the heavy pole skyward. With the hook swaying back and forth, I would battle hard to attach it onto the window latch. Finally secure, one would push or pull the window with a satisfying thump. Job done.

The primary school back then consisted of the Headmaster and a single teacher for each year group. There were no such things as teaching assistants. There was no school secretary and the only other persons aboard were the 'dinner ladies.' Each class had its own designated teacher who dominated his/her allocated room with absolute authority. In this one room all teaching took place throughout the year. The only other room we attended on a regular basis was the school hall. It was where we congregated every morning for assembly which always included singing hymns to the accompaniment of the school piano. 'Onward Christian Soldiers' and 'Jesus Loves Me' were favourites of mine and I sang both with gusto and pride.

The hall was also used to serve school dinners which I tried to avoid at all costs. Unfortunately though, my mother's sister was the head cook and sometimes my mother would be called into the school to help out in the kitchen if anyone was off ill. This meant I suffered the all-too-common fare of creamy potatoes awash with gravy; followed by rice pudding with strawberry jam mixed into it. I feel sick just writing about it.

Discipline was tight and punishment was usually administered via a cane or a 12" wooden ruler to either the hand or buttocks. There was an armoury of punishments, with each individual teacher having his/her own favourite. Pieces of chalk or wooden board rubbers flew around the classrooms, sometimes connecting with unruly pupils. I remember one teacher who would have the unfortunate trouble maker stand in front of the class on just one leg for the remainder of an entire lesson. That happened to me once. Sometimes a troublemaker would have to stand in a corner and wear a dunce's cap... a tall conical creation made of paper and with a letter 'D' emblazoned on it. Fortunately, I can't remember ever wearing that.

During my last year at primary school I was in the charge of a teacher whom I shall call Mr. Davies. He was a tall, ram rod straight man who always wore a dark blue pin striped suit. He either looked after this suit very well or he had several identical ones tucked away at home as his mode of dress never varied. Generations of pupils who passed through his hands will testify to this suit. It became famous in its own right.

Mr. Davies was a strict disciplinarian and was keenly respected by us all. He kept a traditional school cane tucked up one or other of his sleeves. At the slightest observed misdemeanour by any of us, he would withdraw this cane in an instant and smash it down on the desk of the guilty pupil with a resounding crash. No pirate or any of the three musketeers could have drawn their swords quicker.

One particular morning there was a loud knock on the heavy wooden door that led into the class room. A junior pupil nervously entered. He was clutching a piece of paper which was dully presented to Mr. Davies. A hush fell over us all as he read the note in silence. What was all this about I thought? Dismissing the messenger with a flick of his hand, Mr. Davies began to read out aloud its contents.

"Will the following boys report to Mr. Jenkins's room immediately," he bellowed in his baritone voice. 'Someone's in trouble?' I thought. Mr. Jenkins was the Headmaster of our primary school. He, more importantly to myself, was my father's uncle. He was a nice and kind man but one who would willingly punish those who deserved it.

Mr. Davies began to read out the names of those on the note. I, myself, was feeling somewhat relaxed as, after all, I was a *good* boy and *never* got into trouble! Besides, I always felt an air of immunity due to the close family connection between Mr. Jenkins and myself. After all, he *knew* I was a good boy…didn't he?

My confidence grew as it became evident that the boys on the list of names solely consisted of the usual and well-known trouble makers of the class; boys with whom I rarely associated with except out of fear. Name after name was read out until, to my utter disbelief and shock, I heard mine. I took a mental double take as the cold surge of terror gripped me. I, indeed, was one of the summoned few. My world began to spin and my stomach heaved as I slowly rose from my seat and, in a daze, headed towards the door.

Six of us had been summoned and we made our way slowly and silently across the playground to meet our fate, good or bad. I tried to remember if I had done anything wrong but nothing came to mind. Absolutely nothing. Some, like myself, were lost in their panicked thoughts whilst others, unconvincingly, shrugged off the news by acting as if they were gangsters and didn't care.

In a conspiratorial group we hesitated outside Mr. Jenkins's office, daring each other to knock. Amongst many crossed whispers someone eventually rapped his knuckles against the heavy wooden door.

"Come in," the familiar voice commanded. We all filed into the room, the gangsters of our small group suddenly devoid of bravado. The smell of wood polish invaded my senses. Mr. Jenkins was leaning forward in his chair writing. Without even the slightest glance in our direction he ordered the door closed and for us all to move forward. We all shuffled across the hard wood parquet floor; tinted a dark brown by age, polish and countless small feet. We formed a rough semi-circle in front of his desk. Above him, high on the wall, a portrait of Queen Elizabeth looked down at us. To my young eyes, she seemed disappointed in us all. Behind us the large round clock ticked away the awkward seconds. My legs began to feel as if they would soon give way.

Mr. Jenkins suddenly flung down his pen and leant back in his chair. Finger tips steepled, his eyes roamed over us like a searchlight traversing across a prisoner of war camp, just like in the war films I had seen on television. The conversation that followed went something like this...

"Well boys," he paused for effect. "I have had a very serious complaint concerning all of you." Another pause. "I have just had a phone call from Mrs. Gwyn."

Further explanation as to the identity of Mrs. Gwyn was not needed. She was the Headmistress of the village infants' school; from which all of us had left five or six years earlier.

Even though time had passed, the mere mention of her name sent a cold memory through my thoughts. We had all passed through her clutches. I can picture her now. A hawkish thin woman with hair tied back in a severe bun. She was a hard disciplinarian and woe betide anyone who stepped out of line when she was around.

"Mrs. Gwyn," Mr. Jenkins continued. "Tells me that you boys were seen playing in the infant school's grounds over the weekend. Apparently, you were seen climbing trees and kicking a football about."

At this point I had better explain that playing in the grounds of the infants' school was strictly forbidden, not without the permission of a teacher anyway. In fact, it was a rare treat to even get to walk on the grass, let alone climb trees. As such, playing there on a non-school day was absolute taboo and if caught, one would have to suffer the consequences. Ironic really as time has revealed. These days the building is the village community centre and use of the grounds is highly encouraged.

"This is a very, very serious offence boys. So serious that I do not really know how to handle it." Mr. Jenkins paused for thought. "I know," he suddenly exclaimed in a flash of inspiration. "I'll ring Mr. Davies the village policeman and ask his advice. He will know what to do."

This was devastating news for all of us. Constable Davies was at least nine foot, twelve inches tall and a man who, according to my mother, regularly put naughty children in jail! Most villages, including Penclawdd, had its own police station with incumbent police constable. He made it his business to know everybody, especially the local villains. He, like teachers of the day, was a highly respected member of the local community and feared by those of us still in short trousers. If I really had to pass him in the street, I straightened myself up and displayed my best behaviour. We all did.

"Good Morning Mr. Davies," I would chant, only to be given a cursory nod and a quick up and down inspection in return. How times change eh!

With a flourish, Mr. Jenkins picked up his big black telephone and dialled a number. He held the ear piece to his ear and listened intently. "It's ringing boys," he said in triumph. "It's ringing." The clock seemed to tick more loudly. "Ah! Is that Constable Davies the village policeman?" he enquired. "Oh good. It is you Constable. This is Mr. Jenkins here, the headmaster of the junior school."

In my mind's eye I could see Mr. Davies sitting at his desk in the police station. "Oh! I am very well Constable Davies. How are you?" Another second or two ticked by. "Oh. That's good. And Mrs. Jenkins is very well too. Thank you for asking. How is Mrs. Davies? Oh she's fine as well. Excellent!" Mr. Jenkins took on a more earnest tone of voice. "Now Constable Davies. I wonder if you can help me. I have some boys here who were seen playing in the grounds of the infants' school over the weekend." I could almost hear the voice that replied. "I agree with you Constable Davies. It is a very serious offence. I have just been telling them that." Mr. Jenkins emphasised the word *very* as if it was the longest word ever.

"What is the punishment for such bad behaviour then Constable?" Mr. Jenkins paused and nodded his head several times as he took in the answer. "Good grief," he said in shock to no one in particular. "Good grief," he repeated. "Jail is it Constable Davies? The boys will have to go to jail?" Mr. Jenkins looked shocked. "When will they have to go to jail then?" He listened intently and shifted in his seat. "I see. They will have to go to jail over the summer school holidays?"

At this point in proceedings one of our number fell to his knees on the wooden floor and clasped his hands as if in prayer. "Please Mr. Jenkins," the boy pleaded, trying bravely to hold back his tears. "I can't go to jail. My father has booked a caravan at Port Enon for two weeks. I can't go to jail." The pitiful plea was quickly dismissed with a sharp wave of a hand. "Mr. Jenkins," another boy croaked with trembling voice. "I would rather pay a fine than go to jail."

"Constable Davies," Mr. Jenkins continued. "I have one boy here who wants to pay a fine instead of going to jail. Is that allowed?" He looked the boy straight in the eye. "How much money have you got Constable Davies is asking?"

"Two whole shillings." The boy almost cried, his body trembling.

"He's got two whole shillings Constable Davies. Hmmm. I see. Not enough, is it? He will have to go to jail with the others, will he?" The Headmaster nodded a few times as the conversation continued.

"Constable Davies," he said with a questioning tone. "Some of the boys here are quite upset by the fact that they will have to go to jail. Is there any other suitable punishment?" The nodding continued as Mr. Jenkins listened carefully. "I see," he said several times. "I see. I can give them the cane instead, can I? Once across each hand?" He nodded sharply. "Thank you, Constable Davies. You have been a great help." Relief flowed over me. The cane was bad enough but at least I wasn't going to go to jail. None of us were it seemed.

The big, black telephone was replaced in its holder with a bang. "Well boys. Line up and stick out your hands, palms upwards." Mr. Jenkins rose from his seat, picked up a twelve-inch wooden ruler and stepped forward. One by one we shuffled forwards, my eyes flinching with the sound of each thwack of wood against flesh. I was last in line and soon only Mr. Jenkins and I were left. He hesitated and looked me in the eye. For a fleeting moment I thought my close family connection might save the day, but no such luck. A minute later I was shuffling back to class blowing onto my cupped hands in a vain attempt to ease the sting which radiated from the red welt that ran across each palm.

*****

As a footnote to this story, I, later in life, became a teacher myself and spent twenty-five years in the profession. Over that time I have often recalled that day when all six of us were summoned to our fate. I have often wondered too, whether or not Constable Davies was, in fact, on the other end of that telephone conversation? Or was it a brilliant piece of play acting by Mr. Jenkins? What do you think?

By the way. Most of us were back playing in the Infants' School grounds the following weekend. So there!

THE END

Did you know...
That the term 'corporal punishment' derives from the Latin word *corpus* which means *the body*? It was banned from British state schools in 1986 and was allowed up until then because teachers were seen as authority figures; having the same rights as parents via *loco parentis*.

BURNING ONE'S BRIDGES

A railway line ran through the village of Penclawdd where I grew up. At least there *was* a railway line until Doctor Beeching had his way back in the 1960's. Following his big shake up of the railway system throughout the country our village railway line, like many others, vanished; destined to become in later decades, cycle paths, footpaths, bridleways or simply left to rot. The railway through the village was spanned by four bridges. I say *was* because following the events I am about to tell you about, there were soon only three.

Three of the bridges were testimony of the stone mason's art. Built from dressed stone they boasted small stone corner turrets at each end. The bridge concerned with this story, however, was the ugly duckling of the four. Apart from the two stone-built support walls which held back the steep earth banks, the entire edifice was built of wood with an earth covered roadway forming its span. It had no safety rails flanking it at all.

As a young boy I never wondered why this bridge was so very different in design from the other two. In later life though and considering the bridge's generous width and the complete absence of steps at either end, I concluded that it was probably built to accommodate the horse and donkey drawn cockle carts that were a common sight in the village back when I was a boy. I may be completely wrong on this point of course. but it seems a reasonable explanation as to why the bridge existed.

The supporting timbers of the bridge were a latticework of very large and heavy beams approximately two feet square and many feet in length. Following the demise of the railway, several attempts were made by local rascals to burn these timbers. I remember that such activity was readily evident by many of the timbers being blistered and blackened by smoke and flame. The bridge though had been built to last and, as such, defied all attempts to destroy it. That is until the day I am writing about. On this day it became evident that the phantom arsonists had struck again, this time with some success. My attention had been roused by my mother.

"There seems to be a fire over there," she announced from the kitchen. "Over by the old bridge." I ran to the back door and stepped outside. Sure enough. Thick wafts of billowing black smoke were curling upwards from the general location of the bridge. My young ears pricked up at this. Smoke meant fire and fire was exciting.

"I'll go and see," I shouted at my mother. I rushed the few hundred yards to the bridge and close inspection revealed that one of the main upright supports had almost burnt through. 'Wow,' I thought. 'This is great.' Red embers waxed and waned at each caprice of the breeze whilst the black, tar - stained smoke billowed from the innards of the beam itself.

Whilst I was staring, fascinated at this smouldering mass a small gang of older boys (who shall remain nameless) arrived. They too, had been alerted by the billowing smoke. Ignoring me, they set about trying to make this defiant bridge support part company with mother earth. I watched in awe and wonder as they hurled boulders onto the smoking weak spot. My anticipation escalated as the whole bridge shuddered at each impact; resulting in small avalanches of dry, dusty earth to shower upon us from the roadway high above. Slowly I eased backwards, trying to divorce myself from what was happening. This was serious stuff that was going on.

This bombardment of rock against wood continued for some time; my excitement of what might happen heightening with each passing minute. Eventually the support beam capitulated. A long, drawn-out groan of tortured timber rent the air. Virginal white wood appeared as the beam split and finally parted.

As fast as my legs could carry me, I fled from the scene and took up a safe position some hundred yards distant. The onslaught of boulders continued until the bridge, with a violent shudder, began to slowly twist and sink. The lads underneath dropped whatever rocks they were holding and fled in gleeful panic towards where I was standing. I continued watching, unable to break my gaze away from the final moments of this long-standing structure. Subconsciously, I stepped even further backwards.

The air filled with the loud screech of parting timber as the whole bridge roadway began to tilt towards me. An avalanche of earth cascaded in a dusty waterfall as the bridge, at last, relented to the force of gravity. Clouds of dust billowed skywards and rolled along the line of the old railway track towards where we were all standing. The cacophony of noise as giant beams bounced off each other would, I was certain, be heard throughout the village. Especially at the police station which was only a few hundred yards distant. A flush of panic gripped me as I imagined blue flashing lights and police officers appearing from everywhere.

Without a word to each other, we all scattered in various directions. I ran home via a roundabout route and walked up the side path of the house to the kitchen door as nonchalant and as innocent as I could possibly look. The rest of the day I spent playing in my bedroom, not daring to venture outside.

Even though I had not actually participated in the destruction of the bridge, I did keep a very low profile for several days and hardly left the house. Every day I was fearful of the heavy knock of authority on the front door, soon to be followed by the booming voice of constable Davies, the village policeman. A few days later my mother was preparing my tea when she raised the issue of the bridge.

"I see that the old bridge has collapsed," she said casually. My stomach rose to my throat.

"Has it?" I replied whilst feigning surprise. "I didn't know that."

"You were down at the bridge the other day, weren't you? The day we saw all that smoke?"

"Err yes," I replied whilst thinking hard. "But it was ok then though," I said excitedly, gaining confidence. "Some boys had lit a fire underneath it, but I didn't hang around there too long."

She looked me in the eye as she flicked a tea towel. "You had nothing to do with it then?"

"Not me," I lied. "Maybe the fire burnt the wood holding the bridge up?"

"Maybe," she replied with a questioning tone. "Maybe it did." She disappeared into the kitchen and I breathed a sigh of relief.

As time passed and no one had arrived to cart me off to jail, I took it upon myself to venture along to the scene of the carnage. The dust had long settled and had coated the tangle of beams with a white, frosty looking sheen. Sadly, what had once been a proud bridge now looked defeated and very dead. Oddly enough, one defiant beam still spanned the deep chasm below. It was one of the two main beams which spanned the gap and had supported the cross timbers of the roadway. For years afterwards people used this single two-foot-wide beam as a precarious short cut to the lower village, my mother included. I used it myself many times with complete confidence and oblivious to the dangers. Walking along it became second nature.

Ironically, the very first house I ever bought many years later was right on the site of that old bridge. Sometimes whilst lying in bed, my thoughts would return to that day. I would remember the sound of groaning timbers and the hiss of earth as it cascaded downwards like water. I usually ended up feeling sad for the less of an 'old friend'. In its time it had, no doubt, served the village well.

THE END

Did you know…

When I was a young lad, it was a common sight to see a convoy of horse and donkey drawn, flat bed, two wheeled cockle carts parade through the village. The carts were either on their way out onto the sands or returning from them, laden with heavy sacks of cockles. Many families made their living from this industry and, as I remember, either sold their produce by selling from vans around the local areas or on stalls in Swansea market.

The horse and donkey carts are long gone now and have been replaced by land rovers and tractors. At the time of writing, two modern factories in the village are all that remain of the industry. Most of the produce these days leaves the factories in refrigerated lorries to be sold both domestically and in Europe. I remember very well going out onto the sands with my mother and other relatives to collect a bucket or two of these cockles. Back then, there were plenty of cockles to go around. They made a lovely supper.

DODGING A BULLET

I can't remember a time as a young boy when there wasn't an air rifle knocking about the house. It belonged to my older brother. It seemed that as a young teenager he pleaded with our parents one Christmas for an air rifle. Well, Christmas morning arrived and he and I rushed downstairs to the front room where all the presents were stacked in a neat pile, including our traditional Christmas stockings which were bulging with goodness knows what. There, awaiting Brian, was a long and narrow cardboard box all wrapped up in Christmas paper. In a state of excitement he tore off the wrapping and found a toy rifle awaiting him and which fired what were called caps.

I suppose my brother put on a brave face in front of my parents but his disappointment was easy to see. As such, one day shortly after Christmas, my father arrived home carrying another long, narrow cardboard box. It contained the real thing. A BSA Cadet air rifle.

The arrival of the air rifle meant that our back garden very quickly became a firing range. In all fairness to Brian, he taught me how to use the rifle and how to shoot. He also allowed me to use it whilst on my own in the garden. So much so that overnight, it seemed, most of my meagre pocket money went on buying lead pellets from the local ironmonger.

Our back garden served as my very own battleground in which toy lead soldiers and military vehicles were massacred many times over; their condition deteriorating a little bit further every time. My plastic model aeroplanes which I had laboured over lovingly were blown apart one by one in imaginary air battles and dog fights. Soon, none were left. My mother's supply of potatoes suffered as well, the tall thin ones doubling as enemy soldiers. The advantage of using potatoes was that they blew apart when hit. Better than a potato though was a beetroot. These were great to shoot at as the red juice that spilled forth when hit looked like blood. These were somewhat expensive though, so I only occasionally sneaked one out from my mother's supply, hoping that she would not notice.

One afternoon after I had got home from school I went as usual, out into the back garden with the air rifle. I had just cocked and loaded it when my mother called out to me that tea was ready. I propped the rifle up against the wall and went inside. I was just about to sit at the table when I noticed that the corner of the kitchen where the rifle usually lived was empty. Remembering that the weapon was still outside in the garden, I quickly retrieved it and stood it upright, as usual, in the naked corner. By now, I had completely forgotten that I had left it fully cocked and loaded. Ready to fire!

Brian, older than myself, always arrived home from school later than I did. Whereas I could easily walk home from the village primary school, he had to catch a bus home from his private secondary school in Swansea. So, there I was, demolishing my jam sandwiches and watching television when he arrived home. Entering the living room from the hallway he dropped his satchel to the floor, flung his school cap onto the sideboard and, as he often did, picked up the rifle. Pointing it at me he shouted "Banzai!" and then squeezed the trigger.

I can't remember which of my senses reacted first. My hearing at the sound of the loud crack as the compressed air forced the pellet out of the rifle's barrel, or my sense of feel as the small, lead projectile sliced through the hair on the side of my head? The pellet missed me by the width of a fly's wing and slammed into the drawer set into the built-in cupboard directly behind me. Stunned silence followed as my brother, my mother and myself froze solid as if someone had pressed the pause button on our lives. Both their faces, as was mine I expect, were blanched the colour of fresh fallen snow,

Who reacted first to the chaos that followed is hard to recall? My mother I expect. I remember her screaming

"Peter," through both of her hands which were clasped, in shock, to her mouth. She rushed towards me, pushed my head to one side and thumbed back my hair searching for injury. There was no blood. Not even a mark. She then let fly verbally whilst stamping a foot on the floor in temper.

"Bloody air gun," she screamed. "I'll have that out of the house. Just you wait and see." She snatched the weapon from Brian's loose grip and disappeared into the kitchen. Brian remained motionless, no doubt contemplating the fact that he had almost shot his little brother. I was still sitting at the table feeling as if I was in a strange dream. Slowly I allowed my fingers to explore the side of my head; still not fully believing what had just happened. I just sat there contemplating how close I had come to serious injury or worse.

Returning from the kitchen our mother barked orders. "Peter. Get out of that chair now." I jumped up in record time. She pushed the empty chair aside and checked the damage to the cupboard behind it. The pellet had blasted its way right through the front of the drawer and had embedded itself inside a pair or rolled up socks.

"Get me your plasticine box," she commanded. Turning to Brian she nodded towards the kitchen. "And you," she directed. "Get me the brown shoe polish and a tea spoon." We both obeyed without comment.

"If your father finds out about this, he'll give you both a good hiding. He'll kill the both of you."

Neither Brian or myself ever admitted it, but my father finding out was our main concern as well. The damage to the drawer had to be covered up and disguised before he got home from work. With great ingenuity my mother carefully mixed brown boot polish with the plasticine until the exact colour match with the drawer was found. She then patched up the damage, smoothing the plasticine with the back of the spoon. The chair was replaced in its usual place and both Brian and myself quietly waited for life to return to normal.

I was watching television when our father arrived home. I broke out in a cold sweat as I heard him enter the hallway.

My mother greeted him in her usual way and I relaxed as she acted as if all was normal. She gave no hint as to what had happened.

Both my brother and myself learnt a valuable lesson about gun safety that day which, no doubt, has stayed with us. I never left a rifle loaded ever again and I am sure that he has never pointed one at anyone else. The incident was hardly ever spoken about again but I know that we both remember it well. Bye the way, the air gun was not thrown away and our father went to his grave none the wiser.!

THE END

Did you know...

Back when my brother, Brian and I were teenagers, the Birmingham Small Arms Company (BSA) was a major British industrial group of businesses manufacturing military and sporting firearms, bicycles, motorcycles, cars, lorries, buses and the like. Founded in 1861, it continued until its demise in the 1970's when all the businesses were sold off. BSA was a name that everyone knew and trusted. It represented *Britishness* and quality.

*****

The BSA Cadet air rifle was first produced in the 1950's and was one of the world's best-selling powered weapons with many thousands sold worldwide. The rifle was of 0.177-inch calibre. The pellets we usually bought from the local ironmonger. They came in boxes of 200 pellets. For half a crown though (about 12.5 new pence), a tin of 500 pellets could be bought. These prices might seem very cheap by today's standards, but all this took place in the 1950's. To add some perspective to this amount of money, my first ever *weekly* pay packet as an apprentice engineer was three pounds and sixteen shillings (about £3.80p in today's money) and two pounds of that I gave to my mother.

'Caps' were very common back in the day and came in small rolls of a waxy type paper which had a row of pimples along its length; each pimple containing some sort of explosive powder. These rolls of caps were inserted into toy pistols and rifles so that when the trigger was pulled, a hammer mechanism struck a pimple, thus creating a sharp crack or bang. I remember that fired caps had a pleasant and distinctive smell, very similar to that of a spent firework or Christmas cracker.

FEELING THE HEAT

High up at the top end of my home village of Penclawdd was the municipal rubbish tip. To us locals, it was simply known as *The Dump*. The dump was located on the site of a long-abandoned coal mine and was a popular playground to many of us adventurous children. Here, the dust carts as we called them, would deposit all the rubbish they had collected from houses in the village and beyond. I am writing here of a time before the concepts of *recycling* and *saving the planet* had even been thought of. There were no black rubbish bags, nor were there any blue, green or pink ones either. All we had back then was the metal rubbish bin into which everything went and which was emptied by the council once every week.... Yes. That's right...*every* week!

Anything that could not be fitted into the bin you took to the dump yourself. As such, this vast area contained a varied mix of rubbish. There were abandoned motor vehicles, bicycles, furniture, prams, toys, ovens, televisions, fridges, electrical goods of all descriptions, all lying there amongst thousands of bottles, tins, cans, cardboard boxes and goodness knows what. It was quite an adventure going there as we could never tell what we might find.

For those of us who had air rifles the dump was a magnet. Brian, my older brother had such a rifle and the both of us had fun times blasting away at the rubbish. There was no shortage of targets. No bottle or tin can was safe. Sometimes my brother borrowed a second rifle from one of his mates so that we had one each. A visit to the tip could account for a tin of five hundred air rifle pellets easily, sometimes more.

It wasn't, however, only inanimate pieces of junk that we shot at. A popular pastime of ours was shooting the rats that infested the dump in their hundreds. We would rarely see any rats during the day but once darkness fell, these little squealers would begin to stir. A rat shoot involved Brian and myself visiting the dump at night. One of us took charge of the rifle whilst the other held a powerful torch. The torch we used had a very powerful, but narrow beam which we slowly traversed across the rubbish heaps like a searchlight in a prisoner of war film. One could hear the rats scurrying about, but as soon as the torch beam hit them, they would freeze. Like rabbits caught in a car's headlights they would stop where they were and stare back. When this happened, all we could see were two yellow eyes reflecting back at us.

At this point the shooter took a steady aim, held his breath and gently squeezed the rifle's trigger… rat dispatched! When up on the dump by oneself the torch was taped underneath the rifle's barrel. This acted like a crude version of the modern red spot laser sight that is seen in many of today's action films. It was very effective though and achieved the same result…dead rats!

One afternoon during school holidays I was up at the dump on my own. I wasn't after rats, though if one appeared it would probably end up very dead. I was shooting at bottles and anything else that I considered to be a worthy target. To me, these bottles and such were the enemy. A foe that had to be beaten and the battle won.

I was standing on top of one of the old coal mine's spoil tips onto which the dust lorries would drive and tip their contents over the edge. The tip's surface was flat, compacted earth but its sides consisted of loose rubbish. I had spent some time collecting a lot of bottles as I needed two opposing armies before battle could commence. I had just finished strategically positioning the bottles when I caught a movement in the corner of my eye.

A dust lorry was coming down the track leading to the spot where I was standing. My pulse raced as I panicked; fearful of being caught by the lorry's crew and being taken down to the police station. I knew that air guns were very unwelcome at the dump as there were stories that broken bottles, left on the dump's dirt roadways, has punctured the tyres of more than one dust cart.

I had been slow in spotting the lorry and I cursed myself for my lack of attention. I desperately searched for a means of getting away, but the vehicle was now so close that all the normal avenues of escape were closed off. There was only one option available. With my brother's precious rifle held aloft above my head, I launched myself off the edge of the tip with a leap of faith. My intention was of running through the loose rubbish down to the solid ground below. As soon as I made contact with the rubbish, my feet broke through and I immediately sank down to my thighs. Horror gripped me as I imagined being swallowed up and my reflexes kicked in fast and furious. Pure adrenalin kept me pushing forward, pushing and shoving; desperate to reach safety and to find a spot to hide away from the men above.

I was halfway down the side of the tip when, whatever it was my feet were pushing on, suddenly gave way. I immediately sank down into the rubbish to chest level. In wild panic I kept pushing forward and entered an area of what must have been buried hot ash. It was not uncommon to see parts of the dump burning or smouldering. Old mine spoil tips often did. They either self-combusted or were set on fire either by boys like myself or by the hot ash described above which had been previously deposited by the bin lorries.

I felt the heat attack me. I was beginning to burn. My only option was to keep pushing forwards. Only panicked instinct was keeping me going. Rationality had long gone. My lips pursed as the searing pain in my legs began to bite. The situation was not helped by my wellington boots filling with hot ash. As I pushed through, red hot embers glowed around my legs. It is amazing what panic and adrenalin can do as I do not remember breaking free from the inferno and stepping onto solid ground. All I was interested in at that moment was staying alive and avoiding being caught. Ahead of me were several high brick walls, once part of some old mining structure. I dodged behind one of these walls and hid from view; my heart pounding as I leant against the cool bricks. 'Please. Please. Please don't let me get caught.' I pleaded to God.

I heard the lorry pull up and the cacophony of noise as a fresh load of rubbish poured down the tip. I could also hear voices but not what was being said. Would the men search for me I wondered or would they ignore me and drive away? Fortunately it was the latter. As the noise of the revving engine began to fade and die away, I began to calm down. It was only then that I took stock of my condition and remembered the hot ash in my wellington boots. I quickly kicked them off and they were soon followed by my smouldering trousers and socks.

Both thighs and lower legs, including my feet were scorched red but I was thankful and relieved that I had not been seriously burnt. Now, exposed to the cool air, my legs began to sting. Grabbing handfuls of cool, wet, grass, I rubbed down the affected pieces of skin for relief. My thick trousers were steaming but had escaped unscathed. The bottom of my woollen pullover though had been singed in several places, whilst my rubber wellingtons had partly melted and would no longer stand upright of their own accord. The socks though, after a good dusting, seemed none the worse for wear. I allowed the clothing to cool for a bit before putting them back on.

Fully serviceable once more, I listened carefully for sounds of other human activity. Had the dust men really gone or were they lying in wait and ready to pounce as soon as I broke cover? I had heard the lorry leave but that didn't mean that someone was not still watching and waiting. There were no noises except for the disturbed rubbish settling down again. The coast was clear. I waited a further minute or two and then trudged off home feeling somewhat sorry for myself. A good, hot bath was needed.

THE END

Did you know …
These were the days before central heating and combi boilers. Houses had coal fires which had to be cleaned out every morning and re-laid with scrunched up newspaper, sticks and coal. I was often given the privilege to light the fire with a single match. I would set light to a corner or edge of newspaper and delight in watching the flames work their way upwards, setting alight the sticks which supported the coal. Soon a steady fire would be burning and kept going throughout the day with the occasional addition of more coal. The old ashes from the previous day's fires, usually still warm, were placed in the metal dust bin ready for the weekly collection.

*****

Today though there is no sign of the *dump*. It was largely levelled and landscaped and is now quite a nice area to walk in.

THE WALKING WOUNDED

The paternal grandparents of Brian and myself lived in a village called Llanmorlais which is about two miles west of Penclawdd where we were both brought up. Their house was the last but one situated on a dirt track road which led up from the level crossing close to the railway station. When Doctor Richard Beeching decided in the 1960's to rip up a third of the United Kingdom's rail network, this railway was one of those that disappeared. The resulting empty area became an extension to our adventure playground with steep, bracken covered banks leading down to where the double line of tracks once ran. Running along the top of each bank were wire fences, two or three stands of stiff wire supported by square cross sectioned wooden posts. These fences separated the railway property from everything else.

On the far side of the railway, and more or less opposite my grandparents' house was some long-forgotten coal mine. The shaft entrance had long been sealed off with concrete and access, thankfully, was denied to adventurous and inquisitive youngster such as Brian and myself. As far as I can remember, the only other visible clues to the mine's existence were a few small spoil heaps, or *tips* as we called them.

These heaps of mining waste had been reclaimed by mother nature and were, in the main, covered with grass, bramble and gorse bushes. One of them even sported quite a large and deep pond at its summit. I found this pond fascinating. The water was always black and evil looking, and goodness knows what was lurking in its inky depths. After all, hadn't I been told that it was bottomless? With wicked excitement I threw many a stone or small boulder into it, my imagination watching it sink and sink to the ends of the earth. Many a sea battle was fought on its surface as well, the fleet of battleships and destroyers all disguised as discarded bottles and tins. These, too, sank into oblivion under a deluge of lead pellets from Brian's air rifle or via a heavy bombardment of stones that might be lying about.

Brian and I were playing in this area during a hot summer's day. I can't remember how old I was but I know that I was still in short trousers, He was on top of the spoil tip where the pond was located and was hacking away at a long length of hazel wood with his long, bone handled sheathe knife. He was fashioning a crude throwing spear. I was down at ground level slicing away at some enemy soldier who had had the audacity to disguise himself as a fence post. I was using a double-edged billhook which I had sneaked out of my grandmother's garden shed. Its normal use was for chopping up logs for firewood.

I was deep in battle and hacking away at my assailant when Brian suddenly shouted something. I didn't catch what he said as the thumping of metal against my enemy's wooden head drowned it out. Again he shouted. "Look out," he screamed. This time I did hear him but as I began to turn my head in his direction something hard, heavy and very sharp slammed into my right calf. Brian's newly fashioned spear sliced into my leg; tearing flesh and muscle to shreds.

Screaming with pain I almost blacked out. As the spear forged its way through my leg, my right hand, the one holding the billhook jerked backwards in an involuntary motion. With a dull metallic thud, the short outer cutting edge sliced into the top right-hand side of my head. Howling with the sharp stinging pain, I let go of the billhook.

Down it fell, landing heavily on the foot of my damaged leg. I hardly felt the impact though as my other wounds were much worse. I remembering staggering about with my eyes closed and fighting back the need to faint and fall to the ground. I flattened my palm against the head wound and felt something warm and sticky flow between my fingers. It was blood. I was in a total state of panic as I felt the ooze run down my face. The carnage to my leg was, for the moment, completely forgotten.

I felt someone grab my shoulders. "I told you to look out you idiot." The voice sounded distant but I knew it belonged to my brother. "Keep Still," he commanded with a jerk to my body. "Let's have a look at you." By now, he, too was in a panic. He forced my head back but why he thought this would help I had no idea. I just did what he said. Following a quick assessment of my injuries, he pulled the spear from my leg, picked up the blooded billhook and rushed me back to the house. Limping along and with head hung low in cupped hands, I trailed a path of blood whilst terrified that I was going to die. Reaching the back door we found it wide open.

"Stay there." Brian whispered urgently. He then let go of me as he walked inside to the kitchen. Holding my head and slowly buckling with fright and pain, I watched him speak to my grandmother who was out of my line of sight.

"Peter has been hurt," he said sheepishly. "He's had a spear in his leg and a billhook in his head." He motioned me inside. My grandmother was sitting at the table shelling peas into a large earthenware bowl. Her mouth dropped as she gazed upon my bloodied form. The fact that I had been wearing a white top didn't help. It was, by now, very red!

Within twenty minutes or so, I had been washed and bandaged, head and leg. I was then dragged down the lane towards the bus stop to be taken to the doctor's in Penclawdd. Brian, looking very concerned and somewhat fearful, followed behind but gave up after a while and returned to the house. I was eventually pulled through the door of Doctor Newton's surgery and pushed into a chair. I flinched with pain as he thumbed both wounds as he examined me.

"Those are nasty cuts," he said matter of factly. "Both of them will need stitches."

At these words I again, nearly fainted. 'Stitches,' I thought. 'Don't they involve needles and thread?' Such thoughts were soon answered as with eyes closed and with my lips tightly pursed shut, Dr Newton injected anaesthetic close to each wound. The sting of both needles quickly faded and with my flesh suitably numbed, he set to careful work with his long fearful looking curved needle. I flinched in fear as he approached me but I never felt a thing. The anaesthetic had done its job well. Even so, I left that surgery with tears rolling down my cheeks. It had, after all, been a traumatic day.

Whenever I have occasion to remember the events as described above, my fingers still, sixty odd years later on, automatically search out one or other of the two scars. Oh yes. I have the scars to prove what happened. I am looking at the one on my leg right now!

THE END

Did you know…

A billhook is very similar to a short axe. It has a short wooden handle and a long metal curving blade which terminates in a kind of hook with a sharp point…hence its name I suppose. The inner edge of the curve has a cutting edge. The tool is a very versatile cutting implement and is used widely in agriculture, forestry and other similar industries for cutting woody material. My grandmother's version though had a short straight cutting edge on the reverse of the blade in addition to the main cutting edge.

JUDGE, JURY AND EXECUTIONER

As mentioned elsewhere in my writings, it was usual when I was a young boy for each village to have its own police station with its very own police officer. Our village of Penclawdd was no exception. Our village policeman was Police Constable Davies or Mr. Davies as we called him. If you have already read my story *Discipline Ain't What It Used To Be,* then you will have already been introduced to him. To me, he was a giant of a man… at least 6' 13" tall… who kept his wary eye on the whole village.

Being a permanent member of the community, he soon got to know who the local rotten apples were and where, if he needed, to find them. He patrolled the village on foot but would sometimes be seen on his sturdy black bicycle. He demanded total respect from us youngsters and he usually got it. If I saw him walking towards me and there was no route of escape, I straightened up, looked smart and greeted him politely.

"Good Morning Mr. Davies," I would chime depending upon the time of day. He, in turn, would turn his eyes sideways and look me up and down and just give a curt nod in acknowledgement. He would then continue on his chosen beat, ramrod straight with both hands firmly clasped behind his back. I remember he once stopped me when I was out riding on my brand-new bike which Father Christmas had brought me.

"Where is your bell?" he queried.

"I haven't got one yet," I replied, my voice quivering with terror. "Father Christmas brought me this bike but it has never had a bell."

"Father Christmas eh," he replied. "I'll have to have a word with him. He should know better than to give young boys bikes with no bells. Perhaps the elves forgot to put one on." I quickly nodded dumbly in agreement, eager to shift the blame onto the elves.

Mr. Davies then went to great lengths explaining to me the importance of me having a bell on my bike and that I could go to jail if it was missing. Finishing the lecture, he actually walked me home with myself pushing my deficient bike alongside me. He explained to my mother the issue at hand, and within a few days my bike sported a brand new; shiny blue bell.

Just as most villages had its own police station with its own police officer, most villages in Wales also had its own rugby pitch. Some even had more than one. Rugby, of course, is the national game of Wales and is both played and supported with great zeal. The rugby pitch in my home village of Penclawdd is known locally as *The Rec*… short for *Recreational* Ground I suppose? The Rec is much more than a rugby pitch. Even today as I write this, it boasts two tennis courts, a bowling green, teared viewing platforms and many years ago, a cricket pitch. All these are lorded over by a fine pavilion located high on the south bank of the field.

I was playing around on the Rec with my brother, Brian and several of his mates. All were older than myself by about seven years. As such, on this particular day I was the odd man out by virtue of my tender years. They were playing at rugby tackling with me being the one being tackled and thrown to the ground each time. I didn't like this at all, but I put on a brave face, complete with false smile. During one of the tackles one of my shoes came adrift, only to be picked up by one of my brother's mates. The shoe was flung back and forth as if it was a rugby ball with little old me pleading for its return.

Brian and the rest of the gang formed a rough circle around me and started throwing the shoe back and forth to each other over my head. By this time I was in tears and screaming for the return of my shoe; my face awash with tears. This throwing back and forth of my shoe continued for several minutes until proceedings came to a sudden stop when a voice boomed across the field.

"You lot. Over here now," the voice commanded. We all turned our heads in unison and saw that the voice belonged to Mr. Davies who, no doubt, had been observing what had been going on. Seeing this authority figure gave me mixed emotions. We were now in trouble, but at least I would probably get my shoe back. Obeying his command I ran over to him as if I was in an Olympic sprint, despite the fact that I was only wearing one shoe. The others followed at a slower pace, hurrying, but pretending in front of each other not to look too concerned. Mr. Davies waited patiently, hands on hips and with the sun reflecting off the polished buttons of his uniform and the badge that fronted his proud helmet. We gathered in a rough semi-circle in front of him whilst catching our breath.

"What's going on here then?" he queried in his deep, powerful timbre.

"They have got my shoe." I replied sheepishly.

"Have they now," His eyes locked on the boy holding the offending footwear. "Give me that shoe." The boy handed it over and quickly stepped back into the safety of the semi-circle of friends.

"Peter," Constable Davies said. "Come and stand here by me." With heart pounding against my chest I did what he bid and rushed over to the protection of his six foot plus frame. He nodded towards another boy.

"You," he commanded again. "What has been going on here? I want the truth."

The boy shuffled his feet and bowed his guilty head towards the grass.

"We have been playing Rugby with Peter's shoe," he confessed.

"Did you have Peter's permission to use his shoe?"

"No," the boy mumbled. "It just fell off his foot."

Mr. Davies puffed out his chest in exasperation. "I see," he said slowly. "So you were all stealing then?" No one replied. "I said," Mr Davies emphasised "You were all stealing. Yes?" One by one several boys nodded their heads. I stepped even closer to Mr. Davies.

He vaguely waved the hand holding the shoe. "Right you lot. Line up on the railing there facing the railway and bend over." *The railing* was the barrier that separated players from the watching supporters. It consisted of a series of concrete upright posts with heavy steel pipes running through them. Resigned to their coming fate, the boys silently complied.

With all boys positioned to his satisfaction, Mr. Davies went into action. At a steady pace he simply walked along the line of his victims whacking each on the buttocks with my shoe as he went. At the last boy in line, Mr. Davies did a turnabout and repeated the process on his way back. Two hard whacks each. He handed me my shoe.

"Put that on and go home straight away. Don't stray anywhere on the way or I'll find out."

I arrived home about five minutes later gasping for breath. I rushed up the stairs and hid in my bedroom awaiting the return home of my brother. I was expecting a slap across the back of my head at least. He eventually arrived but nothing was said and nothing was *ever* said. It was as if nothing extraordinary had happened. I asked him about it recently but he claimed that he couldn't remember the incident at all…yeah!

I kept a low profile for a while trying to avoid the others that were in the group. They might not have been so forgiving in terms of not saying or doing anything. Again though, no one ever mentioned the incident. Perhaps they were too embarrassed?

THE END

Did you know…
During the times when I was a lad, it was usual for each village to have its own police station complete with village police officer. The *village policeman* as he was known, lived at the police station. As well as being his home, the station was his base, complete with cells for those who fell

afoul of the law. Our village of Penclawdd was no exception. The substantial, red bricked building with its blue lamp had its own air of authority and when in its vicinity, I would be on my best behaviour.

When I was naughty my mother often threatened to take me there and have me locked up… the thought of which soon put me back on the straight and narrow. She did actually once carry out her threat. In collusion with the police officer she told him of my misdemeanour of which he was no doubt thoroughly and visibly shocked about. After showing me the foreboding and echoing cells complete with green and white glazed tiles, he let me off with a warning. The building is still there and whenever I pass it by, I often remember being taken there, under protest of course, all those many years ago.

*****

What happened that day described above was rough and instant justice but effective never the less. Police officers back then dealt with minor juvenile misdemeanours in that same fashion. They would spot some mischief, assess what was happening and administer appropriate punishment there and then. They really were Judge, Jury and Executioner all rolled up as one. Can you imagine what would happen to a police officer these days if he/she acted in a similar way? I shudder to think.

THE EARTH REALLY DID MOVE FOR ME

My brother Brian and myself grew up on the northern coast of the Gower peninsula. This coastline can be described as a gentle one as the agricultural land, dotted with small pockets of woodland and areas of open common, give way to tidal marshland and the sea itself. It looks out over the tidal Burry Estuary which separates this northern shore from Carmarthenshire. Gower's southern coast, however, is in complete contrast to its northern neighbour. Its agricultural lands give way to rugged limestone cliffs, sandy bays, secret coves and outcrops of rock that reach out onto the Bristol Channel.

What Brian and myself were doing on this south Gower coast I do not know. We might have been fishing or looking for prawns and crabs in the rock pools? We could have been looking for rabbit holes on the cliff tops for future investigation by my brother's ferret? I really can't remember. I do remember that we did visit the famous Paviland cave but am pretty certain that such a visit would have been a side show to the main reason we were there.

Whatever the reason my brother and myself were in the area, our adventures came to an end and we headed back towards his car. There is a perfectly good path along the top of the cliffs, safe and relatively flat. Brian though, decided that we would take the more difficult and hazardous route along a series of rock ledges that traversed the cliff faces. These ledges varied in width between several feet and a few inches and were more suited to mountain goats than human beings. I was fearful about taking this way back as I was scared of falling. I did not mention such fears though so off we went, me trailing in Brian's footsteps.

Some of these ledges had gaps in them where the cliff face had collapsed into the sea below. These we had to jump across. I approached each of these gaps with dread and with each leap, I was convinced that I was going to die. I remember one particular ledge which had a gap of about two and a half feet in length. Below the gap the cliff fell away vertically to the sea washed rocks far below. My brother jumped the gap with ease and beckoned me to follow; promising to catch me as I landed on the far side.

"You sure you will catch me?" I asked uncertainly.

"Of course I will," replied Brian. "You saw me do it didn't you? It's easy." He pointed at the ground by his foot. "Just jump and aim your foot for there. As you land, I will grab your arm." I hesitated for a few moments, trying to block out the drop below from my mind.

"Come on," Brian shouted. "Jump. It will be ok." I summed up a great surge of courage and took the leap of faith. My foot hit hard ground as indicated and, as promised, Brian caught me and pulled me to safety. I stood still for a moment as I caught my breath and calmed down. In fact, I felt really pleased with myself for having made the jump. I had done something brave and I felt good about that.

As we walked along the ledges, we amused ourselves by kicking or throwing any fairly large stones or boulders over the edge. We revelled in their long fall. These missiles either shattered to pieces on the rocks below with a deafening clatter or splashed into the sea with explosive force…great fun! At one point I noticed a fairly large boulder protruding from the edge of the ledge. Gently pushing against it with the sole of my boot I discovered it was loose and that, with a bit of encouragement, it could soon be hurtling downwards.

I looked for my brother but he had gone ahead and disappeared around a curve in the rock face. I was on my own. In order to gain some leverage, I sat down on the wide ledge with my back against the cliff. Again I positioned my boot against the fated boulder and pushed forward with my leg whilst bracing myself hard against the cliff behind me. The boulder put up a good fight and valiantly resisted my efforts, but it was weakening fast. I kicked and kicked and eventually the boulder gave up the battle and disappeared over the edge. As it did so, the entire ledge that I was sitting upon suddenly moved forward slightly with a sharp jerk. Instant terror gripped me as I imagined the ledge collapsing. I am sure that I must have stopped breathing at that point. Was I going to follow that boulder or not?

Forcing myself to keep calm and very still, I very slowly turned my head to look behind me. The ledge, for several feet either side of where I was sitting had moved away from the cliff face. A dark and narrow cleft had appeared where both had previously been joined together. I sat there motionless, my imagination already seeing me hurtling towards the shore below in an avalanche of rock. Again I looked for my brother but he was nowhere in sight. I was too scared to shout.

Breathing hard to quell my panic, I very slowly placed both hands flat against the ledge below me. Pushing upwards and backwards in small instalments, I slowly moved away from the edge. With each push my senses searched for any movement of the ledge. Had it moved just then? Was it my imagination? Was that the sound of the ledge giving way?

As the seconds ticked away as if long hours, I made slow progress. Finally my back felt the hardness of the cliff face behind, and pushing with my legs, I gradually slid up the cliff until I was standing upright. Looking down at my feet the cleft between cliff and ledge ran beneath my boots. Had it widened or was my imagination playing tricks again?

Keeping calm by taking even more deep breaths, I slowly traversed along the cliff face step by gentle step. I am certain though that the last foot or so was covered in record time! I made it to safe ground, gave a quick prayer of thanks to God and pulled myself together. I continued along the ledge at a fast pace, eager to reach the grassy slopes beyond which heralded safety.

I rounded the last curve of the cliff face and saw my brother sitting on a sunny incline waiting for me. I sat down breathlessly alongside him.

"Where have you been?" he queried. Excitedly I stammered out the recent chain of events. He listened patiently but I wasn't sure if he believed me. When I had finished my tale there was a pause. "Come on," he said as he rose to his feet. "Let's go. I'm starving." That was that!

THE END

Did you know…
Paviland Cave is very difficult and dangerous to access. Reaching it involves either jumping across a very deep and considerably wide rock chasm or traversing a near vertical cliff face. Whichever way one gets there one needs a head for heights. Its original inhabitants would have had no such difficulty. Way back then, tens of thousands of years ago, the Bristol Channel which now laps at the foot of the cave did not exist. The cave inhabitants would have looked out across a vast wooded plain with exotic animals roaming about. Fossilized trees have been found further up the Bristol Channel coast and during excavations of the cave, tusks belonging to long dead mammoths were found.

*****

I returned to that spot on the cliff many, many years later as an adult. That section of ledge was gone. I wondered how long it had lasted before surrendering to the sea? Had it collapsed that same day long ago or had it lasted many years? Had some unsuspecting cliff walker been the final straw?

I looked over the edge down to where the sea crashed over the rocks in a white froth. There were no bones floating about however. I snapped out of the memory, shrugged my shoulders and continued on my walk.

THE FOX DID IT!

The houses where both sets of my grandparents lived had large back gardens which still exist to this day, albeit under new ownership. Such gardens are very common in stand-alone properties of a certain age in both my home area and throughout South Wales as a whole. Back in the day, most of these were what I would call *working* gardens whereby almost every square inch was used to augment the household food supply.

Potatoes, cabbages, carrots, peas, beans, lettuce, onions and the like were grown. As well as these staple foods, some gardens boasted more exotic plants which bore different types of edible berry and fruit. Strawberry, Raspberry, Gooseberry to name just a few. Remember, these were the days long before the invention of the now ubiquitous supermarket! I, for one, am old enough to realise that fruit, vegetables, meat and the like do not, in fact, originate in vacuum packed plastic wrapping!

Both my grandfathers were keen gardeners. They had both spent their lives working underground hacking coal which was used to fire industry as well as homesteads. Maybe their respective gardens provided them with the light and fresh air which they were denied at work? Even so, *The Dust,* as Pneumoconiosis is known, rotted their lungs over time and eventually caused the demise of them both.

I would say that my paternal grandparents had the bigger of the two gardens. This gently led down from the rear of the house and ended up on the banks of a twisting river that snaked its path amongst the trees. The top part of the garden, nearest the house, was devoted to the growing of the staples as mentioned above. It also boasted a small greenhouse and a couple of wooden and corrugated steel sheds; not to mention an outdoor privy which stood alone like a white washed sentry box.

A pathway of stone paving slabs led down the centre of the garden and ended at a tall wire mesh fence with a door set in it. This barrier completely encircled the lower garden, the enclosure within being the chicken run where my grandparents raised and kept a collection of laying hens. These were not kept as pets. The chickens provided meat and eggs for the table and I remember my grandfather dispatching one bird with an axe.

The sharp blade thumped into the wooden block and I watched, completely enthralled, as the bird dropped to the ground and ran around headless until it bled out and eventually fell lifeless. The bird was then dunked in a bucket of water and I was tasked to remove the feathers by hand. The carcass was eventually handed over to the care of my grandmother who took it into her kitchen which contained all of her culinary mysteries. Eventually, the bird ended up on our dinner plates accompanied by potatoes and vegetables from the garden… a completely home-grown meal. Real food!

That central path also led to the *big* greenhouse which was very big indeed. It was accessed from the garden but was built into the chicken enclosure. I can remember that it always had a warm, dusty smell and during the summer months was filled with tall rows of ripening tomato plants. My most powerful memory of that greenhouse though, was the fact that all four internal walls were covered with mature grape vines that snaked skywards towards the light. Grapes, both green and red, hung in luxurious large bunches. What my grandparents did with so many grapes I do not know, but they made a tasty treat when I played in that building. I still love grapes to this day.

I also remember that the entire chicken run was devoid of any grass. No such plant could have survived the constant pecking and scratching of so many hens. It was compacted earth, and during hot summer days became very dusty. Several mature apple trees kept the hens' company, their fruit yet another addition to the household's food supply. This enclosure was a playground in its own right, and I had many adventures whilst playing there, both real as well as pure fantasy.

In a far corner of the enclosure stood the chicken shed. The use of the word *shed* seems unkind really as it was quite a well-built brick structure which, like the sentinel outdoor privy, was whitewashed. This is where the chickens laid their eggs and roosted at night. I remember that my grandmother had several porcelain eggs which she placed in several of the nesting boxes. These were supposed to encourage the hens to lay the real things. Whether or not these decoy eggs worked their magic I do not know, but I still have one of them on display in my study. As was my fancy in my boyish mind, this building became a fort, a ship, an aeroplane, a mountain and goodness knows what. If it still exists today, it probably still bears the scars.

My brother was playing around in the chicken enclosure with his air rifle. As usual, there were plenty of hens about, scratching and pecking at the dust searching for any grains of corn left over from feeding time. Strutting about amongst them was the one and only cockerel. The bird pranced about showing off, making his dominance over the hens very evident. My brother was watching this display of arrogance going on and, acting on a whim, pointed the air rifle in the general direction of this brazen creature. "Take this you cocky bugger," he said as he pulled the trigger.

He had, of course, only intended to frighten the bird. Instead though, he couldn't have fired a better shot if he had sighted on the cockerel with a telescopic lens. There was a loud *thwack* as the pellet made contact with the bird's neck. It dropped to the ground lifeless.

Horrified, the young assassin ran over to the feathered heap. A quick examination confirmed that the cockerel had met his maker and a quick look around determined, thankfully, that there had not been any witnesses. My brother, overcoming his panic, came up with a plan. A few guilty days passed before the question he dreaded was put to him.

"Have you seen the cockerel?" Our grandmother asked him. "I can't see it anywhere. I haven't seen it for a few days."

"No," he replied with the most innocent voice he could muster. "I haven't seen it either."

"Let's go and look for him then," said our grandmother.

What was going through my brother's mind as they both walked down the garden path I don't know, but I guess he knew that crunch time had come. A diligent search was made in and around the chicken enclosure. Every bit of the mesh wire fencing was inspected for holes and every tree, bush and nook and cranny was forensically looked at. No cockerel was forthcoming.

My brother casually wandered to the outside of the enclosure where the river flowed. "Here Nana," he shouted with false excitement. Here it is. It's in the river." An inspection was made from the high river bank. Sure enough, a sodden lump of feathers lay in the water. It was identified as the missing cockerel right enough.

"How on earth did it end up there?" Our grandmother said to no one in particular.

"A fox must have taken it." My brother replied excitedly.

"A fox?"

"Yes. A fox," he repeated. "There has been one around here lately," he lied. "I've seen it a few times. It must have grabbed the cockerel and dropped it when crossing the river."

"Hmm." our grandmother mouthed suspiciously.

"Yes. A fox must have taken it," he repeated. "The fox did its Nana."

Nana accepted the explanation, but I think she knew differently though. Don't you?

THE END

Did you know…

A male fox is called a 'Dog Fox' or 'Tod' or even a 'Reynard,' whilst a female fox is known as a 'Vixen.' Young foxes are known as Pups, Cubs or Kits. A group of foxes is called a 'Skulk' or a 'Leash.'

*****

Foxes can produce a variety of noises but the most distinct is a chuckling type sound called a 'gekker. Foxes will gekker when fighting, playing, excited or nervous. As foxes are nervous animals, they emit the gekker sound quite often.

ADVENTURES IN STEAM

In several of my stories I have mentioned the steam railway which ran through my home village of Penclawdd. This railway line terminated in the village of Llanmorlais where my paternal grandparents lived. In my younger days the line was used for the storage and shunting of open and covered wooden built railway wagons. The wagons would come and go as needed, but often stayed parked outside our grandparents' abode for many weeks at a time. They were great to play around with and such a wagon made an excellent den.

The railway was part and parcel of everyday life. It was common place to see these great black leviathans puff their way through the village under a forced cloud of pure white steam. Indeed, the tracks and the trains themselves were a natural, but officially forbidden extension to our playground. If we happened to be on the tracks when a train appeared, we simply stepped aside and stood still as the engine and its accompanying train of wagons sped by, sometimes only inches of fresh air separating them from oneself. Sometimes the driver would give a cheery wave as he shot past in a blur of movement. Sometimes one would be completely ignored.

The great clouds of steam were a great source of fun of their own accord. Two of the four bridges that spanned the railway were designed for pedestrian use only. Their roadways were made of wooden railway sleepers laid side by side along a steel frame. As such, there were small gaps between these sleepers which the steam cloud blasted through as the engine passed underneath. It was often a race to reach the nearest bridge before the engine did. Standing directly over the tracks, we would delight in being completely engulfed in warm steam as the engine rattled through, its pistons hissing and thumping with raw power.

Brian, my older brother taught me how to modify this game by attempting to drop large stones down the train's funnel as it past under the bridge. Success at this required skill and timing. As we could not see anything but white steam, we had to guess the right moment to release the stone which we held over the parapet. We scored a few successes but usually we missed our target. The misses were immediately evident by the clang of stone against metal as the stone bounced off the engine's casing. They were also evidenced by either the driver of fireman leaning out of the engine and shaking a fist at us. Fortunately, by the time this happened, the train had travelled a fair distance so we were never recognised. Good fun!

*****

Like many boys did back in the day, my mates and myself laid old penny coins on the polished rails when a train was due through. Under the crushing weight that passed over them, the pennies would be squashed flat. This resulted in a thin disc of a diameter considerably larger than the original coin. These made excellent miniature throwing discs or *Chakrams* as I believe they are properly called.

Chakrams are a type of throwing weapons from the Indian subcontinent. An old English term for them is war-quoit. The circumference of each of these discs was sharpened to a fie cutting edge and could be thrown either vertically or horizontally at an enemy. This is how we fashioned them but I remember Brian coming up with the idea of filing pointed teeth around the circumference so that the disc ended up looking like a circular saw blade. Such teeth would allow the mini chakram to stick into the target. I spent hours in the shed at home, my squashed pennies firmly clamped in my father's workshop vice as I busied myself with a small, thin file. As we had no hordes of invading armies to fight, the wooden doors of the shed, outside privy and garage soon bore the scars of battle. So did the trees that grew in the locality. I can't remember us lads throwing these at each other, but we probably did…ouch!

*****

Another crazy game we played was to allow the train to run right over us. I don't mean that we laid prostate across the tracks like some kidnapped damsel in distress; so often seen in those old black and white silent films. Instead we would lie beneath the rails inside a concrete drain pipe.

Brian and I were visiting our paternal grandparents and were playing around on the railway about a quarter of a mile away from the railway station. Where we were, a farm track crossed over the railway. We were happily minding our own business when we heard a train approaching. Looking up line we could see the powerful tell-tale cloud of steam appearing over the low-cut hedges that bordered the tracks. We could have easily walked to safety along the farm track in either direction, but my brother had other ideas. "Quick," he said excitedly. "Follow me."

Running parallel to the track was quite a deep and overgrown ditch which, I presume, had been dug to divert water running off the fields opposite. This water, in turn, would drain away through a series of underground pipes that ran under the railway track and at right angles to it. These pipes were buried about a foot or two below ground and extended the full width of the tracks, Any water would drain away down a steep slope which eventually led to a narrow river.

My brother jumped into the ditch which, fortunately was dry. I quickly followed wondering where on earth we were going. My brother dropped to the ground and began to disappear inside one of the drainage pipes.

"Come on," his echoing voice commanded. "Get in here quick."

It was a tight squeeze, but after brushing aside the dewy nets of silky cobwebs, I managed to crawl after him, the muddy soles of his boots inches from my face. The pipe was bone dry but, even so, had an almost overpowering smell of damp and rotting vegetation. The smell was sweet. In the near distance a circle of light marked the other end of the pipe and freedom. My brother stopped crawling. "Wait here," he said. "Wait whilst the train runs over us."

"Will we be ok?" I nervously asked. "What if the train breaks through and crushes us?"

"Don't be daft. The train has run over here thousands of times. It hasn't broken through yet." I just lay there, not totally convinced. A knot of fear formed in my stomach.

As we were underground, the thumping of the approaching train seemed to be all around us. I could hear the metal rails above us start to sing. Our protective pipe began to vibrate, causing dust and encrusted dirt to fall on top of us. Spiders scurried about whilst unrecognisable bugs crawled sedately through the thin layer of black dirt that lay beneath us.

The sounds of the rattling and hissing train reached a deafening crescendo which invaded every part of my body. Terrified, I buried my face against the curved face of the pipe and closed my eyes. The vibrations increased tenfold, evidenced by the rattling of my teeth through my cheek bone. I lay there in a state of terror wishing that it would all stop. I was totally convinced that the train would break through and that we would, indeed, be crushed to a pulp.

The noise began to abate as quickly as it had begun. The thumping of the pistons and the blasting of steam replaced by a continuous and repetitive rattling as the train of wagons passed overhead. We could sense that the last wagon had passed by when the sounds began to fade into the far distance. Peace soon returned.

"Come on. Let's go," my brother said.

We crawled through the dirt and cobwebs and out of the far end of the pipe. We dusted ourselves down and went about our business again. I repeated that experience several times, either on my own or with some of my mates. Even so, my only memory is of that very first time. I guess it was the most frightening because it *was* the first time. One didn't know what to expect and because of that, I suppose, it seemed all the more adventurous and dangerous!

*****

Talking of danger, I imagine that the most dangerous of our adventures with steam was the cadging of lifts on the train. As stated above, my paternal grandparents lived in the next village down line and where the line itself terminated. If either Brian or myself wished to visit our grandparents then we usually walked there, caught a bus or in my case, cycled.

Another way of travelling to Llanmorlais was to jump onto a passing train when no one was looking. This method of quick and effortless travel was first introduced to me by yes, you've guessed it…Brian, my brother. I was never enamoured with this mode of travel as I thought it far too dangerous. In fairness, I don't think my brother used it much either; probably for the same reason.

The technique involved hanging around the railway station at our home village of Penclawdd. Usually, the trains stopped here as part of railway business. If it was a long train of wagons, we would stealthily walk along the side of the train which could not be seen from the station. We would be looking for an enclosed wagon that had its large, wooden sliding door unlocked. Finding one, my brother would climb in and pull me up after him. We then closed the door and wouldn't open it again until the train moved and was well away from the station.

Sometimes we would clamber into an open truck. This was more difficult as these had no doors and we would have to climb up and over the truck's side. These trucks were no good if it was raining as we would be exposed to the elements. Good fun though on sunny days. We would lie there on the wooden floor gazing skywards, watching the long snaking trail of thinning steam scar the pure blue sky above.

The most precarious method of travel though was reserved only for occasions when no such trucks could be accessed. This involved climbing up onto the buffers which separated two adjacent wagons. We would sit on a buffer as one would sit on a horse with legs either left dangling into space, or wedged against the wall of the truck opposite. This was a rocky ride, but we soon got used to the rhythm of the swaying trucks and adjusted our bodies accordingly. A few feet below us the ground and railway sleepers rushed past in a blur.

The train always stopped at the station in Llanmorlais, which gave us time to alight from our hiding place. It was then just a case of sneaking along the line of wagons on the blind side of the station and avoiding the train crew. We were never caught.

On one occasion I was with Brian and a mate of his. They were both older than myself and thus bigger and stronger. As the train pulled out of Penclawdd station, my brother and his mate ran after the last wagon and grabbed onto an end buffer each. They climbed up and sat facing backwards. I was running hell for leather after them as they both reached out an arm to me. "Come on," Brian shouted as he beckoned me on. "Hurry. We'll catch you and pull you up."

To whose offered hand my eager fingers locked onto I cannot remember. I had a good grip but my young legs could not keep up with the ever-increasing speed of the train and I let go. I stumbled forward, tripped over a railway sleeper and went sprawling across the rails. Cursing, I sat with grazed knees just in time to watch the train diminish in size with its two rear seated occupants waving goodbye to me. I gave up on going to Llanmorlais that day and stumbled home instead.

"Where is your brother?" my mother asked as she tenderly rubbed Germolene antiseptic cream onto my knees.

"I don't know," I replied. "I think he might be walking down to Llanmorlais."

THE END

Did you know...

Chakrams originate from the Indian subcontinent. Primarily designed as a throwing weapon, chakrams were also worn in the turban in order to protect the head from sword attack. Smaller variants were worn on the arms and wrists and used like knuckledusters. Worn on the arms they could be used to cut into an enemy during hand-to-hand combat. Worn on the turban, they could be used to inflict injury on an opponent's head of face or whilst grappling. A modern-day toy which is based on the Chakram's aerodynamic design is the plastic Frisby.

TIME AND TIED WAIT FOR NO MAN

If you have already read my piece above entitled *Where I Lived...My Home,* you might already be familiar with my description of the tidal salt marshes that sit opposite the village where my brother and I were brought up and lived. Needless to say, these marshes can be dangerous for the unwary and many people have been caught out by the fast-rising tides and difficult terrain. A maze of meandering rivers, carved out of the mud by the ebb and flow of timeless tides, can make the marsh a hostile place to be. These twisting rivers are known as *pills* which vary greatly in terms of length, width and depth.

All of his life my older brother Brian has been interested in shooting, fishing and other related sports. He particularly enjoyed the challenge of duck shooting, most of which he did on these local marshes.

On an incoming tide, once the rivers and pills fill with water, it spills over the banks and travels faster than one can walk. Over the years there have been several occasions when cockle gatherers and fishermen have been caught out by this fast tide and paid the price for doing so. One has to keep an eye on the tides and the amount of water running in the tidal river that parallels the shoreline of the village. My brother and his mates from the shooting fraternity were no exception for the need to carefully scrutinise the tides.

One winter's day, he and several of his mates had ventured out on the marshes on a duck shoot. They were all local lads except for an invited guest. This guest was a Swansea based millionaire who had recently taken up the sport of shooting. Most of the lads had their trusted gun dogs with them, all trained to retrieve any fallen ducks, especially if they landed in the water. The monied guest was no exception and had his dog by his side. It was a very expensive black Labrador and was, no doubt, his pride and joy.

Several ducks were shot, but the last one to fall fell into the tidal river on the northern edge of the marsh. The guest's dog leapt into the water and swam in pursuit. The mud brown swirling tide was fast flowing into the estuary. Both duck and dog were soon caught by the strong current and swept up river. The local lads were getting concerned about the tide and were itching to head back to the shore which was a good mile away to the south. The millionaire though, concerned for his dog insisted on waiting. So they all waited, their apprehension of the rising waters increasing by the minute.

The delay continued and my brother, having been watching the rising tide, turned to one of the others. "We've had it," he muttered. "We'll never get back in now."

At long last dog and owner were united and the party set off to cross the marsh to safety. As my brother had predicted, however, they had left it too late. Even though they were walking across dry grass, the rising tide had filled the pills ahead of them and the water was soon spilling over the muddy banks at a fair rate of knots. The pills soon disappeared from sight, lost to the rising waters that were crawling relentlessly over the grass towards the shooting party. They were forced to stop in their tracks and think of what to do.

With a soft and sibilant hiss, the waters soon reached the boots of their waders and menacingly circled their feet. Within minutes they could see no solid ground around them. With the pills hidden from view it was impossible to navigate a path to shore. To move forward was dangerous as one might suddenly disappear from view into several feet of water. The local lads had a good idea as to the height of the tide that day, so the decision was made to stay put until the waters finally peaked and then abated.

The water slowly crept up their waders and the shortest member of the group was the first to feel the discomfort of cold water pouring down inside them.

"What's it feel like?" he was asked.

"You'll soon bloody well find out for yourself," came the irritated reply.

Another problem was the welfare of the dogs. Unable to stand on solid ground, they began to tread water and swim around in scraggy circles. This state of affairs could not be allowed to continue, so the dogs were picked up and slung across the shoulders of their owners. To add to the drama the sinking sun finally dropped over the horizon and darkness fell.

As they all patiently waited, a series of distant blue flashing lights were observed rushing through the blackness and along the main road. The lights seemed to belong to police cars and fire engines and the group were left wondering what sort of a drama was going on in the village. A serious road accident perhaps? The lights disappeared from view but soon returned in the opposite direction.

They stopped more or less in direct line with the suffering group who soon realised that the emergency services were there for them. Then gunshots were heard coming from shore. Someone was trying to communicate with the party and answering shots were fired back. Such communication was repeated several times throughout the dark evening with each answering shot meaning 'We are ok.' Luckily, before the early winter darkness had fallen, the plight of the group had been spotted by two other wildfowlers who were further up the marsh. It was they who had alerted the emergency services.

To the relief of all concerned the tide eventually stopped rising when it was waist deep. According to my brother, the group stood rooted to the spot for approximately three to four hours, their bodies chilled to the bone. At long last the waters receded to a point where it was safe to move their aching limbs and start the journey back to shore.

Stepping off the marsh they were met by a throng of people. Not only were the emergency services present but also the local press. Each person was checked over medically and given a tetanus injection before being briefly interviewed by a reporter. I still have the press cutting in the family photograph album. It is a short piece and to the point. No doubt if someone had died then it would have had a much bolder headline.

When my brother Brian stepped ashore, a bottle of liquid was thrust into his hand. "Drink this down boy," a voice rasped. He gulped the contents gratefully. It was not until a short time later when my brother started laughing and singing, that it was realised that the bottle had contained whisky. Not being a great drinker, he soon became *rat-arsed*. The last he can remember of that evening was being stripped naked by his wife and his mother and thrown into a hot bath. No doubt he wasn't singing and laughing the next morning though … a million tiny hammers pounding inside his head maybe? Serve him right.

THE END

Did you know…
Fog and mist are another hazard out on the marshes and one could easily lose one's sense of direction if caught out in such conditions. I was once told that if I was ever caught out on the marshes by fog or mist, then a trick to find safety would be to follow the sheep tracks in the grass. These might lead me on a roundabout route, but would eventually get me ashore. Sheep and horses seem to be able to 'sense' the way to safety. Sometimes animals know best.

LOST IN TRANSLATION

Those of you who might be around the same age as myself, might remember sitting the 11-plus examination during your last year of primary school? I wish to explain that, as expected by my parents and teachers alike, I failed it dismally. For those younger readers who may not know what on earth I am talking about, please read the *Did you know* footnote below. I will say here though, that success or otherwise at this examination dictated whether or not one attended either a Grammar school or Secondary Modern school respectively for one's secondary education.

I plodded through my school years doing no more or no less than was asked of me, and was probably classed as *Could Do Better.* During my final year at secondary school, however, I somehow managed to pass an examination allowing me to attend Technical College, full time, for one year in order to study engineering. There, I took off academically like a rocket. I had found my niche. The practical application of subjects such as mathematics and science really opened up my mind. At last these torturous subjects became relevant and meaningful.

The engineering curriculum was a pretty heavy one which included Mathematics, English Language, Engineering Science, Technical Drawing, Mechanical Workshop, Electrical Workshop, Physical Education and a strange and alien subject called Liberal Studies. This was very different from our other *heavier* subjects.

We had a very good lecturer whom I will call Orwig. He went to great pains to introduce us uncultured engineering students to literature, poetry, public speaking, politics, local history, amateur dramatics, map reading and camping as well as more practical issues such as how to open a bank account, write a cheque, use a library, get a mortgage, buy a car and the like. Orwig encouraged several of us to pursue the Duke of Edinburgh's Silver and Gold awards and for the latter, my parents and myself were invited to Buckingham Palace where I proudly received the medal.

On the strength of that full-time year of study, I was offered an apprenticeship by a local manufacturing company. It was not the end of college though, for I was sent back there on day release for every year of my apprenticeship in order to build up my skills and qualifications. Liberal Studies was still there, year after year. I found the subject interesting but its only downside was that it was always held in the evening after a hard and heavy day of engineering related subjects.

Orwig was still the lecturer and he and I got on very well. When I reached my seventeenth year, Orwig took me aside and asked me if I would like to go on a student exchange visit to the then Czechoslovakia. The trip would take place the following year and twenty-two students from colleges across South Wales would be invited to go there. After speaking to my employer requesting the time off work and to my parents who would help fund the trip, I accepted this opportunity to travel abroad for the very first time in my life.

Before the trip itself, all twenty-two of us students attended a weekend at a South Wales venue known as Dyffryn Gardens. This weekend away was to allow us students, as well as the adults who would be accompanying us, to get to know each other. I can't remember much about that weekend, but as all us students attending were in our middle teens and full of hormones, the time at Dyffryn was probably spent in checking out the opposite sex and falling in love several times over?

Soon, all twenty-two of us, armed with our brand-new passports were all winging our way to the city of Prague. The trip was in two parts consisting of one week in Prague itself, and the second week at an international youth camp attended by similarly aged youths from across Europe.

Whilst in Prague, the capital city, we were all staying in a large hotel which had a very spacious and well-appointed lounge. Here we would gather during our free time and sprawl amongst the comfortable arm chairs and sofas. One particular evening a very smartly dressed young man got talking to us. He was a native of Prague and a few years older than any of us present. His name was Karl. Tall, blonde and blue eyed, he looked very dapper in his double-breasted blazer, shirt and tie. Smart, brown cotton trousers with creases that would have cut through flesh with ease, together with highly polished brogue shoes completed his ensemble. He made the rest of us look and feel like tramps.

Speaking excellent English, he explained that he was very interested in the fact that we all came from Wales. He had heard of Wales but admitted that he knew very little about the country. Sitting amongst us he listened and asked many questions as we began his Celtic education. He was particularly interested in the fact that Wales had its own language; which we all boasted about to great effect. Karl was suitably impressed upon hearing Welsh being spoken amongst our group, and we all had great fun as he tried a few tongue twisting words himself.

As the evening wore on, Karl gravitated towards me and we talked together about all sorts of things at great length. At that age I was still a pretty shy individual, but Karl had an easy way about him and soon I felt very relaxed in his company. He explained that he was studying languages at university and was hoping to eventually gain a doctorate degree. Eventually it came time for him to leave, but before departing he asked me a favour.

"Peter," he said. "I wonder if you would like to visit my home tomorrow evening for a meal and to meet my parents? We could talk some more about Wales." I wasn't particularly keen to take up the invite, but being only eighteen, innocent and naïve, I had no real option other than accepting his offer.

"Yes," I replied trying to sound convincing. "I would like that."

"Good. I will meet you here at five-o-clock. Is that alright?"

"Yes," I nodded. "Five -o-clock will be fine."

The following evening I sat in the hotel foyer hoping that Karl would not turn up. Such hopes were soon dashed though as he confidently walked into the hotel exactly on time. He gave a cheery wave and beckoned me over to the doors that led out into the busy street. Thinking back, I find it quite amazing that I didn't tell anyone in my party where I was going. Incredible foolishness really.

Stepping outside the hotel and onto the walkway, Karl beckoned me to follow him. "Let's cross the street," he said as he took charge of the situation. "We will take a tram. Our home is only ten minutes away."

Within minutes we had dodged the traffic and boarded one of the many trams that trawled the streets of Prague. We trundled along the main thoroughfare with myself secretly noting prominent landmarks. These, I thought, would be useful in finding my way back to the hotel if, at any time, I needed to do a runner. After about a ten-minute journey we alighted, crossed the road and approached a non-descript block of flats. He pointed towards the building.

"Here is where we live. Right up on the top floor." I gazed upwards to the top of the five-story building. I nodded a reply and followed Karl inside. We walked into the spacious foyer and entered one of those open lifts that looks like a cage. One only sees them these days in old black and white films. No solid walls. Just a latticework of metal bars with a bi- fold sliding door that the occupant opened and closed themselves.

The lift rattled and shook its way upwards and stopped with a jolt at a grey and utilitarian landing. Karl's apartment was directly opposite, and as we entered, we were immediately met by his aged parents. Dressed in what must have been their best clothes, they nodded greetings with broad and pleasant smiles. Neither could speak a word of English but with hand gestures I was ushered into the living room.

The apartment was larger than I expected and the dark and well-worn furniture reminded me of my grandparent's house back in Wales. At one end of the living room was a large wooden table surrounded by four matching chairs. The table groaned under the weight of plates and bowls of food, most of which I had never even seen before, let alone tasted.

One thing that has stuck in my mind to this day was that the food was laid out on an exquisite and delicate white lace table cloth. It matched the pinafore that Karl's mother wore over a severe, black, ankle length dress buttoned up to the throat. His father looked splendid in a well pressed dark suit with collar and tie. Both looked and acted somewhat formal, but seemed genuinely pleased to meet me. They had obviously gone to a great deal of trouble on my behalf.

Directed to a deep armchair, I sat down and accepted a cup of coffee whilst Karl explained that the food that we were all about to eat was traditional fare in his country. The coffee was thick and disgusting, but I delicately sipped through it with a forced smile. The food was not much better either but, to be fair, back in those days I was a very fussy eater. I just sat there and ploughed through it whilst answering all sorts of questions from Karl concerning Welsh food and culture. He patiently translated my answers to his parents who sat directly opposite me and who politely listened and smiled. Neither could comprehend a word of what I was saying until each of my utterings was explained to them. Grasping the meaning they would laugh and nod enthusiastically as they waited for the next translation. The meal over and done with, I was ushered back into the armchair.

"Peter. As I told you, I am a student of languages. You, coming from Wales can be of great use to me." I sat there wondering what he was getting at.

Rummaging around in an old cupboard he produced a large, old fashioned, reel to reel tape recorder and placed it upon a small table just in front of me. Seeing this machine the penny soon dropped as my stomach did a turn for the worst. He was going to want me to say something in Welsh. Sure enough, Karl handed me a large and bulbous microphone and a book. I glanced at the book's title to find that it was the novel Ivanhoe written by Walter Scott. I realised my worst fears when Karl next spoke.

"Please would you translate the first chapter into Welsh Peter?"

You might be wondering why I was so fearful of this perfectly reasonable request? I was fearful because, back then, I could not speak a word of Welsh! Alarm rushed through my veins and my face flushed hot and damp. Having spent a large chunk of the previous evening boasting that Wales had its own language, I couldn't very well admit that I couldn't speak it myself? "Yes," I replied awkwardly. "I will do my best."

As Karl pressed the record button on the antiquated tape recorder, my guardian angel suddenly sent me a brainwave. I quickly glanced at the three expectant faces and opened the book to page one. With as much confidence that I could muster I began my translation.

"Mae hen wlad fy nhadau yn amwyl i mi. Gwlad beirdd a chantorion enwogion o fri."

Now. Those of you in the know will recognise the above words as the Welsh National Anthem, called *Hen Wlad Fy Nhadau,* meaning Old Land Of My Fathers. It was the biggest chunk of Welsh that I knew having had it drilled into me since my earliest school days. I went through the words and verses slowly, pretending that the translation was difficult. I also had the prescience of mind to include pauses and voice inflections as if I was reading a story and not reciting a song which, in fact, I was doing. I repeated this several times, breaking up the verses and adding new pauses and inflections.

Then I moved onto Welsh hymns that I had learnt at Sunday School such as *Calon Lan* (Pure Heart). Nid wy'n gofyd bywyd moethus. Air y byd na'l beriau man, and *Ar Hyd_Y Nos* (All Through The Night). Holl amrantau'r ser ddywedant. Ar hyd y nos. Exhausting my knowledge of hymns, I then started on complicated sounding place names such as Llanybydder, Machynlleth, Llanfihangel, Penmaenmawr, Aberystwyth, Pontardullais and, of course, not forgetting the famous fifty-seven lettered Llanfairpwllgwyngyllgogerychwyrndrobwllllantsiliogogog och.

Next came Welsh Christian names such as Angharad, Bethan, Heledd, Gruffudd, Sian, Ieuan…and so it went on and on. Any Welsh word that came into my head was included. All put together in a mix of credible sounding sentences. The minutes ticked by and surreptitiously turning several pages at a time, I eventually arrived at the end of the chapter. Slapping the book shut in triumph I smiled at Karl.

"Job Done," I said confidently.

Karl reached across the table and switched off the tape recorder. "Thank you, Peter," he said with genuine gratitude. "Thank you for translating that. The tape will be an important part of my studies and be a valuable contribution to my collection of language recordings, though I will have no hope of pronouncing those Welsh words myself," he grinned.

"As much hope of me pronouncing your language," I replied. We both laughed and he shook my hand, thanking me again. It seemed that I had pulled it off and had fooled everyone. Following another disgusting coffee I said my farewells to Karl's parents and he and I retraced our previous journey as he escorted me back to my hotel. Thanking me again at the foyer entrance, we shook hands once more and he disappeared into the night. I never saw or heard from him again.

I have often wondered if he ever presented the contents of that tape recording to his university examiners? I shudder at the thought!

THE END

Did you know…
For those of you readers who might have never heard of the 11-plus examination, please allow me to explain. This examination was sat by school children when they were in

their last year of primary education; usually at the age of ten or eleven. Success or otherwise at this examination determined whether or not one spent one's secondary education either in a grammar or secondary modern school.

Grammar schools were perceived as being solely for the *brainy* children who, via an academic curriculum, would be prepared for university and other great things in later life. Those of us however, who went through the secondary modern system, experienced a much more diluted academic programme. On the plus side though, we were taught useful and practical life skills. It is hard to believe these days, but such practical subjects prepared female pupils to become housewives and mothers whilst us boys were steered to become factory fodder or tradespersons. We boys were taught subjects such as Woodwork, Metalwork, Technical Drawing and Agricultural Science whilst the girls did Sewing and Needlework, Cookery and to us young males, the mysterious subject called Domestic Science!

Many thought this binary system of education was socially divisive and looking back from my own personal perspective, I suppose it was. The segregation of pupils into very different educational systems ended friendships of many years standing and we, in the secondary modern system, did feel socially inferior to those who went to grammar school. The system was gradually phased out to be replaced by the more egalitarian comprehensive system. The 11-plus examination eventually passed into history.

JAMMING UP THE WORKS

The year was 1955 and I had been on this earth for nearly six whole years. Liking my own company best I tended to keep myself to myself, especially at weekends. This weekend though was different. It was Sunday and my brother, older by seven years, had been jabbering on about someone called James Dean having been killed in a car crash. That wasn't it though. *This* Sunday was unusually different.

I had been woken up by my mother a good half an hour early and had been washed and scrubbed in the old tin bath on the kitchen floor to within an inch of my life. This over sensitivity concerning cleanliness on a Sunday wasn't unusual in itself, as my sibling and myself were sent off, prim and proper, to Sunday school. There were no religious connotations to this. It was just that it gave our parents an hour's peace to do whatever grown - ups did.

Yes. This was indeed very different. There had been lots of fussing about. Carpets had been cleaned. Furniture polished. Brass candle sticks shone like lighthouses and chairs lined up as if on parade. By mid-morning no trace of dust could have been found anywhere.

"What's going on Mum? Why all the fuss?"

"We have visitors coming today," she replied as she checked me over. She leant closer to me. "And you, young man, had better be on your best behaviour." I looked at my brother with a question written across my face. He just shrugged his shoulders and rolled his eyes as if bored with the whole thing.

"Are we going to Sunday school?" I asked.

"No. Not today. You are both staying home." I was delighted at this news as I hated going. Sunday school was alright in itself, but I just didn't like all the fuss that proceeded the event. Made to look squeaky clean and dressed in one's best clothes.

"Now you go and play but don't go outside or you'll get dirty," my mother continued. "And don't touch anything you shouldn't."

I ambled off wondering what to do with myself and entered the middle room.

Here, a large, polished Queen Anne table ruled over everything else. Usually it had a large glass bowl in its centre, but this Sunday it was covered with a virginal white table cloth, smoothed perfectly flat by gentle and patient hands. The cloth was almost lost beneath plates laden with home-made sandwiches and saucer shaped jam tarts. My eyes were instantly drawn towards these tarts as, at that age, I had an insatiable sweet tooth. Seeing my delight, my mother pointed an index finger towards the table and, with a knowing look, she spoke very quietly.

"Don't you dare touch those jam tarts. People will be calling later and the tarts are for them." I raised my sunken chin from my chest and slowly nodded in compliance.

"Yes mum," I half whispered.

"Good. Now go upstairs and play."

I mooched about in my bedroom doing this and that until boredom set in. At a loss for something to do, I idled down the stairs and arrived back in the middle room. Again, I was confronted by those gleaming and perfectly formed jam tarts and temptation got the better of me. I had the room to myself so, with my senses heightened, I scooped up a handful. I took one from each plate and adjusted the others to cover up the offending gaps. I then ran excitedly into the front parlour to devour my loot in secret. Not being that keen on pastry but addicted to strawberry jam, I licked the tarts clean so that no trace of jam remained.

I now had an immediate problem though, namely what to do with the now empty pastry cups? I looked around the parlour and considered several hiding places. A strange, large wooden box covered with a white cloth sat on a table just behind the front windows. As much as I tried, I could not reach the top of the box. Using the nearby piano stool as a step ladder, however, I eventually gained access. Feeling under the cloth I discovered to my delight, that the box had no lid. The incriminating pastry cups quickly disappeared inside and after rearranging the cloth I placed the piano stool back to where it usually lived. As the day wore on, I eventually forgot all about my crime.

Over the years though and especially at family gatherings and the like, I have been constantly reminded of what I had done. It was my mother who usually told the story. With everyone listening intently she would recall how, on that long-ago Sunday, she had escorted the very first of the relatives and neighbours into the front parlour.

"Imagine the shock and despair of the visitors and myself," she would assert. "When I pulled back the shroud of my father's coffin to find him lying in state covered in jam tarts? There he was, lying in his best suit with two tarts on the top of his head and another perfectly balanced on his chin."

Amidst all the laughter all I could say in reply was, "Oh crumbs."

THE END

Did you know…
Viewing the deceased before the actual funeral was a common thing before the whole business of death became institutionalised. From what I have read, the practice dates back thousands of years. It allowed family and friends to say their last goodbyes at a personal level and also served to remind everyone attending of the inevitably of death. The viewing process varies greatly depending upon religion and culture. In Wales, and probably elsewhere, mourners would often bring gifts of food and flowers.

*****

I remember seeing my mother's body laid out on a table. I wish I hadn't though as seeing her cold and lifeless is my last memory of her. When my father passed, I refused to see him. I wanted my last memory of him to be one of when he was alive.

A REAL CLIFF HANGER

My only personal connection with this story is that I am the one writing it and that I know the two people involved. The two people are my older brother Brian and a very good friend of his at the time whom I shall refer to as Alden. The tale was told to me by my Brian himself. The location of events is a small, sandy cove situated very near the north west corner of the Gower peninsula in South West Wales. The cove, known as Blue Pool Bay, is not that far from the village where my brother and myself were brought up and takes its name from a natural rockpool.

The rockpool is situated at the eastern side of the bay and, at low tide, is separated from the sea by a sandy beach. It is quite deep and is a popular spot for locals and tourists to practice their diving skills from the surrounding rocks.

For those of you who might have already read *The Earth Really Moved For Me*, you will already know that the north coat of the Gower peninsula has very few cliffs compared to the southern coast. What serious cliffs there are tend to be located in this north west corner, though I am sure that several locals would argue the point for there are several outcrops of limestone elsewhere along the northern shoreline. A stretch of high cliffs starts at Blue Pool Bay and extends westward. These cliffs end very near the island of Burry Holmes and an area known as Spanish Rocks, such named presumably, after some shipwreck or other.

Blue Pool Bay itself can be accessed either from the cliff path above via a steep and somewhat unstable path or, at low tide, by walking around a minor outcrop of rock from adjacent Broughton Bay. As a point of interest for those of you readers who do not know the area, at the western end of the bay is a natural rock arch known locally as Three Chimneys. Both the arch and rockpool are completely submerged by the high, spring tides.

As two teenagers, what my brother and Alden were doing in the area I do not know. This story however, involves them both climbing the cliff face from the beach. They were trying to reach a seagull's nest and were probably interested in the eggs that might lie within.

Using just hands and feet and a complete disregard for danger, Brian and Alden started their climb. My brother was in the lead with Alden close behind. The higher they climbed the harder the climb became and eventually a point was reached, just below the nest, which involved a slight overhang. Determined to reach the nest, Brian grabbed hold of an outcrop of rock with his right hand and put his weight on another outcrop with his foot. Pushing against this flimsy outcrop in an attempt to gain a higher hand hold, the rock broke free from the cliff face and clattered to the jagged rocks far below.

His full weight went onto his right arm and his only connection with the cliff face was between his right hand and the spur of rock that it was wrapped around. The momentum of the fall caused him to swing away from the cliff like a clock pendulum. His body reached the extremity of its arc and then retraced its path back towards the cliff.

He tried to grab the rock face but his free hand just clutched at thin air. Horrified, he realised that on the next swing out he would never be able to reach the cliff face and would be left hanging there by one hand. His fingers would slowly lose their tenuous grip and he would fall to his certain death. Just as the second swing was to commence though, he felt a hand lock onto the belt of his trousers. Thinking quickly, Alden had assessed the dire situation and realised that he had one chance, and one chance only, to grab my brother. Luckily his fingers found Brian's belt and slowly and carefully, Alden pulled him in until new foot holds could be found. Both retreated, somewhat shaken I expect, back to the beach. The seagull's nest remained undisturbed.

Brian must have had the fright of his life for he recently told me that of all his adventures, the incident at Blue Pool was the closest that he ever came to meeting his maker. He also told me that he could still visualise the rocks far below and could, if asked, be able to describe each one in great detail. What lesson he learnt from that particular adventure I don't know. You'd have to ask him yourself. The perilous adventures we shared in later teenage years though makes me think if any lesson had been learnt, it was soon to be forgotten!

THE END

Did you know...
I know that many of you will be horrified at this, but egg collecting or bird nesting as it was also known, was a very popular hobby indulged in by many a young boy back in the day. As a teenager Brian was a keen collector of wild birds' eggs and, as I remember, had a very impressive collection with all the eggs laid out in a large shallow cardboard box which was lined with cotton wool. Not wanting to be left out, I even had a small collection myself at one point. My interest was not that great though. It was a fad that soon passed as I moved onto other hobbies and pastimes.

*****

The proper term for egg collecting is Oology which is derived from the Greek 'oion' meaning egg. The practice is now illegal in most jurisdictions. From what I have read, here in the United Kingdom it was first outlawed in 1954 by the Protection of Birds Act and by other Acts of Parliament since. Quite rightly so as well!

*****

Depending upon which reference one uses, Blue Pool varies in depth from about eight feet to twenty-four feet. Its diameter is roughly twelve to fifteen feet. As a very small boy I was told by my father that it was bottomless; something I believed for a long time afterwards until common sense eventually kicked in.

FEET OF FLAMES

I wonder if any of you readers have heard of a substance called Carbide? Its proper name is Calcium Carbide and when I discovered it as a young teenager, I thought that it was the best substance on the planet. When Carbide is in contact with moisture it gives of Acetylene gas which, as you probably do know, is a very flammable and explosive gas. By the way…What *is* the difference between flammable and inflammable?... I *really* don't know.

My brother first introduced me to Carbide. I followed him out into the garden where he showed me a small brown paper bag. Inside were a collection of what looked like small, dusty stones. They were dark grey in colour and, at first, I thought they might be some new kind of sweet. Nearby stood a metal bucket two thirds full of water.

"This is called Carbide," he said. "Now watch this." Reaching into the paper bag he withdrew a handful of this strange stuff and dropped it into the bucket. Amazed, I watched the water immediately begin to bubble and boil. "Stand back," my brother said as he produced a box of matches. Lighting one he threw it into the middle of the cauldron. The effect was tremendous. With a loud *whump* and a flash of white light, the water exploded into flame. 'Wow!' I thought. 'This is pure magic.' Eventually the fire died down and the flames flickered out.

"Give us a go," I cried. My brother handed me the bag. I repeated the experiment with the same effect. From that moment I became hooked. Back then, as carbide was still being used in lamps, it could be freely bought from any ironmonger shop. These days it is classed as a hazardous substance and its sale is heavily restricted. No way can you now buy it over the counter as I did.

As soon as I could, I was spending my meager pocket money at the village ironmongers. In exchange, I was handed a brown paper bag containing the precious stuff. I was also a repeat customer and soon I became something of an expert in producing minor explosions around the village. No pool of water was safe. I remember taking several of my model boats to a local pond hidden amongst several coal waste tips and setting them adrift. Then I dropped in a healthy quantity of Carbide and awaited the water to boil.

Soon, the boats were wallowing about on the turbulent water. I then dropped in the match. The pond echoed to the sudden explosion, the sound reverberating from the spoil heaps. With awe, I watched as the enemy fleet before me caught fire. The models slowly buckled and twisted and, one by one, they either sank or floated as desolate wrecks. Great fun!

Over time my confidence with Carbide grew as well as my complacency. Soon I was chasing after bigger and better explosions. In our garden at home stood my father's wheelbarrow. It stood in its usual spot which was on the rear concrete path that ran along the back of the house. Its drainage holes must have been blocked with dead leaves or mud for it was usually full of rain water. Seeing this mass of water gave me a wonderful but naughty idea. I had recently bought a fresh supply of Carbide and was searching for a new experiment to perform. Clutching my new and bulging paper bag I approached the wheelbarrow.

I emptied the entire contents of the bag into the water which was almost level with the wheelbarrow's brim. The water immediately erupted into a seething white froth the likes I had not seen before. The first pangs of fear clutched at my stomach but there was no going back now. In previous so-called *experiments* I had only used relatively small quantities of Carbide. This was the first time I had used the entire contents of a purchase in one go. The water became so violent that it began to spill over the edges of the wheelbarrow.

I stood well back before throwing the match in a long arc. Instead of the usual heavy thump as the gas ignited, there was one almighty bang that reverberated around the garden. The harsh, white flash blinded me for a few seconds and the heat wave punched against my face. A massive flame shot skyward signing the air with a sooty trail. The return of my vision coincided with the appearance of my mother. Alerted by the explosion she had rushed from the kitchen to investigate.

"What on earth is going on?" she screamed, but her voice dried up as she saw the blazing mass engulf the rear wall of the house.

"I'm only playing with carbide," I said defensively.

My mother just stood and stared, dumb struck by the sight before her. I was now panicking. The fire had got out of control with the wheelbarrow engulfed in flames. Its rubber tyre was burning and was already beginning to melt. I had to put this fire out quickly so, without really thinking, I grabbed hold of the rubber hand grips on the end of the barrow's already hot metal handles and heaved upwards.

The burning liquid cascaded onto the concrete path and like a tidal wave from hell, washed along the path towards where my mother was standing. Sixty odd years later I can still remember her reaction as if it had all happened today. I can also remember that she was wearing blue slippers which were decorated with plastic imitation fur. This fur immediately curled up and melted as the flames washed around her feet. With a high-pitched scream, she jumped up onto one of the steps leading onto the back garden and quickly kicked off her smoldering slippers as soon as she landed.

'Bloody heck,' I thought. 'I am in real trouble here.'

The blazing tidal wave continued its travel and swept around the corner of the house. It passed the door to the kitchen and journeyed down the concrete path that led to the front gate and the public road. Eventually the flames weakened, flickered and eventually died. A heavy silence followed as both my mother and myself contemplated what had just happened. She was the first of both of us to snap out of the muted trance.

"Look what you have done?" she shrieked. "You could have seriously burnt me and you have ruined my slippers." Screaming menace at me she disappeared bare foot into the shed. Moments later she reappeared carrying a stiff bristled sweeping brush. "You stupid, stupid boy." She pointed at the rear wall of the house. "Just look at that young man," she commanded. My gaze followed her finger and I saw a huge, black sooty stain painted onto the pebble dashed wall. "Take this," she said offering me the brush. "I want that wall spotless before your father gets home."

Sheepishly I took the broom from her. Standing on the short wall that edged the back garden I spent a good hour removing as much of the soot as I could. Try as I might though, I could not get rid of it all and the whisper of a stain remained there for many years afterwards. In all fairness to my mother, she never mentioned the incident to my father and he never noticed the stain. He didn't even notice the deformed tyre on the wheelbarrow either. Good job he wasn't much of a gardener!

THE END

Did you know…
I remember my father telling me that when he was a young lad, he had a carbide lamp on his first ever bicycle. Apparently, the lamp had a small tray which contained carbide pellets onto which water was dripped from a reservoir above. The resulting gas travelled along a pipe which led to the burner where the concave mirrored reflector and magnifying lens were positioned. The gas was then ignited using a match or a striker, much in the same way as a cigarette lighter is.

I have discovered since that up until the time when reliable batteries had been invented, Carbide Acetylene lamps were quite common and were also used to illuminate buildings, lighthouses, headlamps of early cars, motorbikes and miners' lamps and the like. From what I have read, these lamps, unlike their rival oil lamps and candles, produced no carbon monoxide, used less oxygen and produced more light. Carbide, apparently, is still used in the manufacture of agricultural chemicals and in steelmaking.

TESTING TIMES

For those of you who might have already read *Lost In Translation,* you will know that I failed, what was known back in the day, as the 11-plus examination. For those of you who do not know what on earth I am talking about, may I suggest that you read that story.

Failing that examination meant that I spent my secondary education in what was known as a secondary modern school. Here we were taught a basic academic programme, but one which emphasised useful practical skills. As well as the usual academic subjects, we boys were taught subjects such as Woodwork, Metalwork and Technical Drawing whilst the girls did Sewing and Needlework and the mysterious subject called Domestic Science!

Personally, I plodded through my school years doing no more or no less than was asked of me but, during my final year at secondary school, I somehow passed an examination allowing me to attend Technical College full time, for one year, in order to study engineering. Here I found my niche. The practical application of subjects such as mathematics and science really opened up my mind. At last these torturous subjects became relevant and clear.

The engineering curriculum was a pretty heavy one which included Applied Mathematics, English Language, Engineering Science, Technical Drawing, Mechanical Workshop, Electrical Workshop, Physical Education and a strange and alien subject called Liberal Studies. This was very different from our other heavier engineering related subjects and introduced us, uncultured engineering students, to literature, poetry, public speaking, politics, amateur dramatics, local history, map reading and camping, as well as more practical issues such as how to open a bank account, write a cheque, use a library, get a mortgage, local history, buying a car and the like.

On the strength of that full-time year of study, I was offered an apprenticeship by a local manufacturing company. It was not the end of attending college for me though, for I was sent back there on day release for every year of my five-year apprenticeship in order to build up my skills and qualifications. Liberal Studies was still there, year after year. I found the subject very interesting, but its only downside was that it was always held in the evening after a hard day of engineering studies.

As one would expect, at the end of every academic year we had to sit examinations in each of the subjects studied. It was a tough examination system back then. Even though the pass mark in each subject was only 40%, if one failed just one of the nine or ten examinations sat, one had to repeat that entire year of study. Yes. Back then one either passed or failed with no resits allowed. Very different to today's gentler grading systems.

I was one of those hyper cautious students who had to revise every scrap of work when preparing for examinations. Some of my peers just studied past examination papers and only revised the appropriate topics, a technique far too risky for my organised mind. I had to revise everything and I can confidently boast that since leaving school, I have never sat an examination without the sure knowledge that I was going to pass it. The examinations themselves were just something I had to plough through, each a three-hour ordeal of continuous writing.

Yes. I put the work in and burnt much midnight oil in preparation. One thing I did object to though, was having to memorize all the complicated engineering and mathematical formulae that one needed to answer some of the questions. My view was that out there, in the real world, if an engineer wanted to calculate something which required a formula to solve, then he or she would look it up from a suitable source, such as *The Engineer's Year Book*. These days an engineer would simply look it up on his/her mobile phone.

As one was not allowed to take such reference books into the examinations and mobile phones had not yet been invented, my devious mind came up with a plan involving cheating. After all, I knew the work backwards so why should I throw away a year just because I could not remember a particular formula? One trick I used was to enter the examination hall with several wooden, twelve-inch wooden rulers stuffed into the inside pocket of my blazer. Each ruler had been carefully prepared with appropriate formula written on them with pencil. I even cut notches into the ends of the rulers so that I knew, by feel, which ruler I needed to take out and crib from… brilliant!

Another trick I used involved the use of what were called *log books*. I am not going to use the next dozen pages or so of this volume describing what these books were all about, but it is sufficient to say that they were thin books with each page full of columns of numbers. If you really want to know something about *logs,* or *logarithmic tables* as they are properly called, then please refer to the *Did you know* section at the end of this story.

Log table books were issued when needed by the college, and during examinations each desk in the examination hall had one placed upon it. The trick was to *acquire* one of these log table books, take it home and staple blank pages into the middle of it. I then simply used these virginal blank pages to write in all the formula that one needed. All I then had to do was to substitute the issued book with the one that had been doctored. The advantage of this trick was that, as log table books were allowed, I could leave it openly on the desk when not needed. I then simply switched the books back again when the examination ended. A great system which I used with confidence. It, and the ruler system served me well over the years of my apprenticeship and I was never caught.

The best 'cheating' scam that I ever pulled off though was during a Liberal Studies examination. I remember sitting at home diligently studying the reams of notes relating to the subject. Remember, that Liberal Studies had to be passed along with all other examinations in order to progress to the next year. I was reading through my notes relating to the Dewey Decimal book classification system that public libraries used. It was not only difficult to take in but was also *very* boring stuff! Bear in my mind, this was at a time when I was in the middle of all of my heavier engineering examinations with my mind already near full of facts, figures and information. I was feeling very tired but then I had a wonderful idea...

At all the examinations that my peers and myself sat, we had to write our answers on lined foolscap sheets of paper with the college's crest at the top of each page. During each examination we could request as much of this paper as we needed. There were usually several sheets left over at the end which I always took home for use as handy notepaper. I had a healthy supply of the stuff.

Our Liberal Studies lecturer had told us that the examination would consist of five questions and, as such, I put my idea into action. We had studied seven or eight topics throughout the year, but which five we would be asked about was an unknown. What I did was to copy out all my notes for each topic onto the college supplied foolscap sheets. I started writing half way down the first page for reasons I will shortly explain. With all topics covered, I smuggled these notes into the examination. The rest was easy. All I had to do was to furtively retrieve my written 'answers' relating to the five topics asked about and use that half empty first page to cleverly (I thought so anyway) relate what each question asked for to my notes as written. This took about an hour and I spent the next two hours rewriting the exam paper over and over again just to kill time. The scam worked a treat and evidenced by a 98% pass mark...A Pass with distinction...Result!

How does that saying go...? "It takes a wise man to handle deceit. A fool should remain honest."

THE END

Did you know…

Log books and the *logarithmic tables* they contained were used to solve various mathematical problems before the advent of electronic calculators and computers. Logarithms convert problems of multiplication and division into much simpler addition and subtraction problems. They were used long before the UK became decimalised which meant that such calculations were far more complicated than they are today. If you are over fifty years of age then you will be familiar with *logs* and *antilogs* as we were all taught how to use them at school. Their use was commonplace and even though very few of us understood them, they became second nature to use.

Logarithmic tables were often referred to as Napier tables after the Scottish mathematician, John Napier, who invented them. He published his discovery of logarithms in the year 1641.

RUNNING OFF THE RAILS

About three miles west of the village of Penclawdd where my brother and myself were raised is the village of Llanmorlais. Here our paternal grandparents lived. This village marked the terminus of the railway line that ran from Swansea and beyond and boasted its own railway station. The wooden built structure has long gone, but the single platform still exists. The route of the line is now a cycle track. Just passed the station the single track morphed into two. Both lines continued for several hundred yards before stopping suddenly at a large pair of buffers. These buffers were positioned just beyond my grandparents' house.

As young lads, my brother and myself spent a lot of time at our paternal grandparents. My brother, older than myself by seven years, spent as much time there as possible helping our grandfather tend the large garden and the chicken run. I really don't remember my grandfather much as he died when I was very young. I do remember though that he had a shiny metal hook instead of his right hand. He had been a coal miner and his lower arm was blown off underground when an explosive charge that was being laid detonated prematurely. He looked like the evil Captain Hook in the Peter Pan stories and to tell you the truth, he frightened me to death.

"Bugger off back to Penclawdd," he would shout as soon as I walked through the door. He would wave his fearsome hook at me. "We don't want your kind down here. Go on. Bugger off home." He was just winding me up of course, but back then I was always looking for reassurance from others that he *was* only just kidding with me.

The mining industry in the area had long finished by the time my brother and I came along. In our day the line was used for the storage and shunting of open and covered wooden built railway wagons. The wagons would come and go as needed but often stayed parked outside our grandparents' abode for many weeks at a time. As such, seeing the steam engines up close was nothing unusual. In fact, the engine often stopped right opposite our grandparents' house and blow its steam whistle. This was the signal for either my brother or myself to duck under the wire fence and scramble down the steep bank to take the offered billy tins from the driver and fireman. Whilst the engine moved off and went about its business, my grandmother would pour fresh tea into the billies and often throw in a slice of homemade cake or a sandwich or two.

As a reward, we would sometimes be given a ride up on the footplate as far as the railway station which was just back down the line. On one occasion I remember both my mother and myself rushing down the lane leading from my grandparents' house in order to catch the bus home. The lane crossed the railway line near where the station was. As we approached the crossing point an engine was shunting some trucks.

"Where are you off to?" Questioned the driver.

"Home to Penclawdd," my mother answered.

"Come on then," replied the driver "We'll be off in a couple of minutes. We'll give you both a lift. Wait up on the platform."

My grateful mum dragged me to the station and we waited. Eventually, the great black metalled leviathan puffed its way to where we were standing. We were both engulfed in a delightfully heat charged white cloud as the engine stopped and released steam pressure. With the help of the fireman we both climbed aboard and soon we were off. The journey was a noisy and bone rattling ride during which I was given the opportunity to blow the engine's whistle several times. Fifteen or so minutes later we arrived at Penclawdd railway station none the worse for our experience. I think my mother enjoyed it. I thought it was brilliant!

One school free day I visited my grandparents with a friend of mine. I will call him Rodger who, like myself, was a native of Penclawdd. He and myself had walked to

Llanmorlais along the railway line, each of us carefully balancing on the rails like tight rope walkers until we lost our balance and fell off. Only to hop back on again and try for another hundred paces before gravity won the game once again.

We finally reached the village and stealthily crept past the railway station for fear of attracting the attention of the station keeper. Officially, no one was allowed on the tracks and this particular station master had a reputation amongst us lads for being a stickler for the rules. I remember he caught me once playing near the station. He grabbed me by my collar and thrust a well-used metal bucket into my hands. Pointing to the giant stack of steam coal nearby he bent down to my level.

"Go and fill this bucket with coal and make sure it's good stuff and not rubbish," he growled. "When done, leave it in the station waiting room." He then gave me a quick clip across the back of my head to speed me on my way.

Roger and myself safely negotiated the station without mishap. Entering what I considered the home stretch of double tracks I was surprised, and a little disappointed, to find each set of tracks empty. As was often the case, our small patch of railway line was devoid of wagons. The shiny rails curved lazily around the bend towards the giant buffers which marked the end of the line. The rails were silent in their emptiness. Empty, that is, except for one odd looking contraption.

Closer examination revealed this stranger to be a pump truck. Now then readers, if you don't know what a pump truck is, I refer you back to old black and white cowboy films or back even further to the silent comic films featuring the likes of the legendary Keystone Cops. In such films you might just be lucky enough to see a pump truck. These track mounted vehicles consisted of a flatbed on which was mounted a device that looked something like a child's seesaw.

On the end of each long arm was a handle which, when pumped up and down by hand, set in motion a collection of cogs and levers which, in turn, turned the drive wheels. It could be operated by one person but with a person at each of the two handles the effort was shared. These trucks were difficult to get moving, but once up and running the amount of power and effort required eased.

Neither Rodger or myself had ever seen a real pump truck before so we both gave it a good close-up examination. We had a good idea how they worked from the type of films described above.

"Come on," Rodger said as he climbed up onto the flatbed. "Let's give it a go." I hesitated for a fleeting moment before joining Rodger. He examined the long-levered hand brake and left it in the 'off' position.

"Grab the other handle," he said. "Let's try and get this thing moving." With both of us pumping hard we soon had the contraption moving at a fair lick of speed. We zoomed past my grandparents' house several times in both directions.

"Let's keep this side of the bend," I shouted. "We do not want to be spotted by the station master. He's a right miserable sod." Rodger nodded in reply.

We soon became embroiled in a test of our combined strength by trying to get the best possible speed out of the truck. So engrossed were we in what we were doing, that it came as a frightening shock to both of us when we heard the whistle of a steam engine.

"Bloody Hell," I screamed. "It's a bloody train!" The loud, mettlesome sound was very close. Sharply turning my head in its direction, I noticed a thick column of steam reaching skywards above the railway bank that hid us from prying eyes. It was obvious that the train was at the railway station.

Rodger slammed on the brake and we skidded to a metal torturing stop. As we stood there like rabbits caught in powerful headlights, again we heard the urgent high note of the steam whistle. Thumping clouds of steam feathered upwards as the engine driver engaged the drive wheels.

With a sibilant hiss, the column of steam began to creep slowly towards us.

"My God," I said to no one in particular. "It's coming our way." In my head and in my stomach, I could see my world coming to an end.

Thinking back to that day, we could have easily jumped off the truck and disappeared over the top of the railway bank to innocent obscurity. Why we didn't do so I have no idea. Instead, we panicked. Without comment, Rodger slammed the drive into reverse and our shoulder and arm muscles bulged as we struggled to get speed up in the opposite direction. It was now a race between us and the engine. Again we shot passed my grandparents' house heading towards the pair of buffers which marked the end of the line. This was where we had initially found the truck parked and, I suppose, was where we eventually intended to leave it.

The engine crested the long bend and came into view. It was dragging a long row of wooden wagons behind it. I had alternate visions of it either catching us up and crushing us to a pulp or us both spending the night in the local police cells. I could clearly see the driver resting on one elbow as he leant outwards for a clearer view ahead. He must have seen us. Our intension was to stop the pump truck just short of the buffers but when Rodger applied the brake, we were travelling at too great a speed to stop in time.

As the defiant looking buffers loomed closer, Rodger shouted "Jump. We are going to crash." Both of us leapt without a further word spoken between us. Rolling in the loose gravel and wild grass that bordered the tracks, we heard the booming metallic impact. I watched as the pump truck bounced violently into the air. Its front wheels remained in contact with the rails but the pair of rear ones came to rest askew on one of the wooden sleepers that supported the track.

The engine had slowed to a crawl but was now very close and spewing noisy unwanted steam in all directions. At this point both the driver and fireman were leaning out to better see what was going on. Regaining our feet Rodger and I climbed through the wire fence bordering the track and vanished into the woods beyond.

I don't know who gave the engine's crew fresh tea and cake that day but it certainly was not myself. Via a roundabout route, Rodger and myself stealthily made our way back home to Penclawdd. I think that I must have kept my head down for a couple of weeks and did not dare to visit my grandparents for quite some time.

The pump truck remained in its distorted position for many weeks but one day it mysteriously disappeared, never to be seen again. No policeman knocked on the door and I didn't spend any time in a cell. With time, I began to forget the incident and became confident that I was in the clear. That illusion though was suddenly shattered when some mates of mine and I were eying up an engine at Penclawdd station. We began talking to its crew whom we all knew by sight. The driver was telling us how fast the engine could go and then his eye caught mine.

"Yes. These engines can go at a fair lick of speed," he explained. "But a few weeks ago I was in a race with a pump truck down in Llanmorlais. If I had had a full head of steam up, I could have caught up with it but, as it was, it just beat me to the finishing line." He gave me a sly wink and the fireman laughed. I'm sure that I blushed red more brightly than any railway signal!

THE END

Did you know…
A pump truck, also known as pump trolley, pump car, jigger, Kalamazoo, velocipede or draisine is a railroad car powered by its passengers operating a mechanical drive system. It was used extensively for railroad maintenance work but also for carrying passengers when needed. They were primarily used from the middle of the 1800's right up until the early 1900's.

It is unclear who invented the pump truck, but it seems that the earlier ones were built my various railway companies from materials at hand, and as such, varied in design. Such trucks were used to transport maintenance engineers and their equipment to where needed on the railway. Later on, various companies specialised in their manufacture and various models of truck were named after the companies that made them, such as Kalamazoo.

Despite films and television giving the illusion that operating such a vehicle was easy, in fact, the pumping action required considerable effort. With the invention of the motor car such trucks fell from favour. Many thousands were built but it is unclear how many survived. Examples can be found in railway museums and some are in private hands.

A LITTLE PIECE OF AMERICA

This is not a story of misadventure as such, but rather one of adventure in a positive sense. An experience which, of its time, was different to the norm. It involved a road trip to a place far away from home and at the other end of the country. I first heard of the trip from my brother, Brian.

"Fancy coming on a clay pigeon trip?" he said out of the blue. "It will involve a two night stay over in a hotel."

"Where to?" I replied.

"To an American air force base the other side of London. You are interested in that sort of thing, aren't you? Planes and all that stuff?"

True, I was interested in 'all that stuff.' A sense of adventure began to stir inside me.

"How we getting there then?"

"There will be eight of us all together, so we'll hire two cars. Four to a car. We can all take turns driving."

"Ok," I said. "It should be good fun. What aircraft fly from this base?"

Brian just shrugged his shoulders. "American ones', I guess? The base belongs to the RAF but the American's use it. It's called RAF Bentwaters and it's in Suffolk, not far from the east coast."

Although I had heard of Suffolk, I had no idea where it was? It sounded a long way away though.

Brian explained that he and several of his shooting fraternity mates had been invited to Bentwaters to participate in a clay pigeon shooting competition. It seemed a long way to go, especially as we had our own clay pigeon club and facilities here at home. Apparently one of the above-mentioned fraternity had a relative working on the base and hence the invite.

I don't know who arranged the accommodation and transport, but I do remember us all picking up two new Mk2 Ford Cortinas' from a car hire company in Swansea on the day of the "off". With guns, ammunition and suitcases safely stored, we started our adventure. Four in each car. We took turns driving and soon this turned into a competition in itself.

For something to do, we decided to see who could drive the furthest in an hour. Being by far the youngest person aboard, I was designated to do all the hard work recording our competitive progress. This was quite easy really. Take the mileometer reading at the start of the hour. Do the same at the hour's end. Subtract the two readings and 'Hey Presto,' distance covered in one hour. I do remember that I won this competition fair and square, even though my calculations were deemed suspect by all.

We made good progress and both cars were performing well until…bang! Puncture rear offside wheel on the lead car. Various expletives were exchanged as both cars pulled onto the road's verge. My brother reckons it was the hard shoulder on part of the M4, but as my memory isn't that good to argue the point, I bow to his better recollection. The boot of the disabled car revealed that even though it contained a spare wheel, there was no jack with which to raise the car in order to affect a wheel change. Examination of the second car revealed the same. Spare tyre but no jack. More expletives rent the air.

There was only one thing to do. Manually lift the stricken car using brute strength. Fortunately, between the eight of us, we had some big and powerful specimens of manhood. Three of the party gripped the underside of the car and heaved. The wheel was very quickly exchanged and on the count of three, the car bounced down heavily on its springs. I stood and watched from a safe distance.

The rest of the journey was uneventful and we made Suffolk in good time. I can't remember anything about the hotel we stayed in. I can't remember its name or even where it was, but we reached it without further incident. We settled in to our shared rooms and after sleeping the sleep of the dead, we headed off to RAF Bentwaters bright and early the following morning.

Each of us were in quiet awe as we approached the base's main gate. An immaculately dressed, white helmeted, shade wearing and armed military police officer stepped out into the road and directed us to stop in a small layby just in front of the barrier. We had only ever seen anything like this in films. I knew he was military police by the large black MP lettering on the front of his shining, white helmet. My eyes took in the immaculate creases on his uniform and the black shine of his boots that mirrored the blue sky.

My gaze rested on his side arm snuggly strapped in its side holster. "Blimey," someone muttered to no one in particular. "A real automatic pistol. Don't annoy him whatever you do." The guard politely checked our credentials and satisfied that we were not enemy agents, directed us to the area where the clay pigeon shooting was taking place.

The designated area of the airfield was very busy. We had never seen so many Americans or heard so many American accents in one place before. In fact, I doubt if any of us had *ever* seen a real American. Many were in military uniform but even those who were not were easily recognisable as American servicemen. Short cropped buzz cuts, immaculate tailoring and an easy-going confidence gave them away. It was a family affair with wives, children and girlfriends joining in the carnival mood. We stood around for a while sucking up the atmosphere and studying the lay of the land. Those in our small group who intended to shoot registered their names. I was there just to watch, listen and learn. The first prize in this clay pigeon competition was some fancy American car. A Cadillac probably. We all commented how great it would be to drive *three* cars back to South Wales.

"Hi guys." Startled, we turned around in unison to the source of this deep American voice. "I couldn't help but over hear you speaking. That's a strange accent you got there. Where you guys from?"

"It's a Welsh accent," someone replied. "We are all from Wales."

"Wales?" The American pondered. "Isn't that where Tom Jones is from?"

We all agreed with knowing nods and various murmurings. Glad to have found a common link with this alien from America.

"Now tell me guys," the American continued. "Where exactly in England *is* Wales?" We didn't know whether to laugh at him, thump him or worse. We soon put him right as regards UK geography though. Even so, I still thought he was confused as to the matter. He shook hands with each of us with great enthusiasm.

"Welcome to Bentwaters guys. Home to the 81st Tactical Fighter Wing, United States Air Force." He introduced himself as an air force Colonel. He pushed forward a shy looking teenage boy. Tall, thin and with the ubiquitous buzz haircut.

"Meet my young son here boys." The lad nodded towards us and gave a shy attempt at a smile. "I am very proud of him. He managed to score an eighty-five today with his 4.10 shotgun." Scoring an 'eighty-five' meant that the young lad had hit eighty-five clay pigeons out of one hundred. "Impressive, eh?" The American continued, patting his son on the shoulder. "I guess I taught him just right.

"Eighty-five," one of our undiplomatic crowd muttered. "What happened to the other fifteen?" The colonel looked perplexed at the question and forced a smile. "Maybe he'll do better next time. See you around guys." He wrapped a comforting arm around his somewhat deflated son and both disappeared into the crowd.

We concentrated on the shooting. Nearest from where we were watching was a young American serviceman in full aviator uniform. Watching him was his doll like girlfriend who looked as if she had just stepped off the set of the American sitcom *Happy Days*. Each time this gum chewing shooter smashed a clay pigeon he turned to his girlfriend as if he was the greatest being on earth.

"Did you see that honey? I blew it to bits."

"You sure did. You are such a great shot honey," she replied excitedly. "You really are so wonderful."

"Tosser." one of our crowd commented. "These guys shoot like robots. Take em out on the marsh back home and the ducks would laugh at em."

"This one wouldn't go," another commented. "He'd be too worried about getting mud on his shiny boots." We all gave a chuckle.

Two amidst our group were very good shots. One was even an international at clay pigeon shooting. One of them I shall call Pugh. Not only was he a good shot, he was a showman. His turn came to shoot and he made a great performance of slowly putting on his skin tight shooting gloves, forcing each finger into place with practiced ease. Next, he nonchalantly took his shades out of his top pocket, flicked them open and put them on. Taking up position inside the safety cage, he swung his gun in a few practice arcs.

"Right," he said to no one in particular. "Let's show these Yanks how it's done… Pull!" The first clay pigeon shot into the air and disappeared in a cloud of black dust, So did the next, and the next. So it continued. Those watching stood in awe as Pugh concentrated through his set. He finished with a quick nod of contempt as he sharply broke his gun. The last two spent cartridge cases ejected and arced to the ground trailing thin blue smoke. Pugh turned towards his captive and silent audience and gave a theatrical bow. He walked off amidst genuine applause and much back slapping.

Our international companion gave a similar performance but without the panache of Pugh. His performance was very business-like. The message had been sent though and it had been received. The Welsh boys had arrived!

Alas, we didn't have time to see the competition through to its conclusion and unfortunately the prize Cadillac remained at Bentwaters. Before leaving the base, we visited the famed American PX shop which every American base had. This is similar to the NAAFI shops on British bases, though NAFFI faded into insignificance compared to this. The PX we entered was a small supermarket and quite alien to us Brits back then. We stocked up on various goodies and I, being in full American mode by now, in deed, accent and swagger, bought a pair of mirrored aviation sun glasses (shades) and a black baseball cap with USAF written across its front in large gold lettering. After all, I needed to look the part.

We arrived back at our hotel looking forward to a relaxing evening. As we entered, we noticed a pile of suitcases and bags piled up in the hallway. It only took a few moments for one of us to clock that they were ours. Our designated leader, the international shot, enquired as to what was going on. The manager quickly appeared.

"I am sorry sir," he said apologetically. "But your party were only booked in for one night. Thus we had to empty the rooms of your belongings ready for the next guests."

"But do you have any other rooms available?"

"I am afraid not sir. We are fully booked up tonight."

Our enquirer whom had made the booking, dropped his head in embarrassed shame and muttered something under his breath.

"However sir," the manager continued. "Realising your predicament, I took the liberty of enquiring with a local Bed and Breakfast establishment not very far from here. Just at the top end of this street in fact. The proprietor has rooms available for you all tonight. Would you like me to ring him now and tell him you'll take them?"

"Yes. Yes please. It is very good of you to help us out this way."

"My pleasure sir. I'll ring him now."

Fifteen minutes later we stopped outside the tall gateway to a large house. The ancient looking wrought iron gates were flanked by two stone pillars, each topped by a fierce looking gargoyle. The house beyond looked as if it belonged in a Hammer Horror film. Ivy clawed its way over the walls and climbed the single turret with its tall, narrow windows. In the centre of the building was a wide set of steps that led to a large, iron studded wooden door. The only things missing were dark scudding clouds, bolts of lightning and clasps of thunder tearing through the air. Our drivers engaged first gear and we cautiously drove between the gates, the tyres of both cars crunching solidly on the gravel driveway. The doorbell was operated by one of those pull-down devices one sees in old black and white films. One of us pulled it hard. We all waited. There was no going back now.

The door slowly creaked open on its old hinges and a man, in his sixties, appeared. He was slightly stooped and had a full head of grey hair. He was wearing a practiced smile. "Good evening gentlemen," he said slowly and with an imagined hint of menace. "I have been expecting you all." Standing aside, he beckoned us inside with a long sweep of his arm. We tentatively entered the hallway. At lease there were no bats flying around or a butler with a bolt through his neck. He led the way upstairs and showed us the two rooms that we were to use. Four single beds in each.

"Once you have made yourselves comfortable gentlemen, tea will be served in the lounge downstairs". He disappeared.

It turned out that he was a very nice gentleman though somewhat eccentric. In the lounge, waiting for us, was his wife and young teenage daughter. We all made our introductions. I thought the young girl somewhat strange in that she looked as if she had just stepped out from some middle ages' fairy tale. She was tall, very pretty with a young, fresh face. A real English rose. Very long golden hair cascaded over her shoulders and down to the back of her legs. She hardly spoke at all and wore a long, loose, white cotton dress that, when she stood up, reached all the way down to her feet which were bare. To me, it looked like a nightgown.

After tea and polite conversation, our host insisted in showing us around the house, which, he assured us, was haunted. We went in every room and the story behind each picture hanging on the walls was told. There were a lot of pictures! With the tour of the house complete, he took us around the large garden. We were invited to enter an outbuilding which stood against the garden's rear wall. Amongst various items of gardening paraphernalia were a stack of yet more paintings. They were originals. Oils and water colours. Our host told us to take our pick of one each as he had no further use of them. We carefully examined them searching for some long-lost Constable, Van Goch or Rembrandt but no such luck. Each of us chose one. Mine has long vanished but my brother, so he tells me, still has his.

I think that evening we ate in a local pub which our host recommended. We eventually retired to our beds, content and happy and recounted the day's adventures. Soon we fell asleep, serenaded into slumber by the pitter patter of tiny feet as mice scurried back and forth across the well-worn wooden floor boards.

Following breakfast the following morning, we were unexpectantly invited to play croquet on the main lawn. I hasten to add that the game of croquet is not very high on the list of past-times in South Wales. None of us had a clue. Our host soon put us right though on the rudimentary rules and his wife and daughter demonstrated the various techniques used to play this gentile game. The daughter was still bare footed and still wearing the same white dress. She had still hardly uttered a word and I wondered for a fleeting moment if she, indeed, was the ghost that haunted the place?

After getting the feel of wooden mallet against ball, we soon had balls sailing through the metal hoops. Unfortunately, one member of our party whom I shall call Alan, had some difficulty with his game. In frustration, he whacked one of the balls as if he was driving a golf ball off its tee. The ball sailed through the air, left the confines of the lawn and decapitated several tulips in a nearby flower bed. The lady of the house looked on in horror. Eventually it was time to leave and we waved ourselves off like long lost family.

I can't remember which route we took back home to South Wales but I do remember that we went via the market town of Cirencester which is situated in the Cotswolds. As we approached this ancient Roman town, I was in the driving seat. I was still in full American mode, wearing my newly acquired mirrored shades and USAF hat. A gaggle of young ladies was spied up ahead. I shifted down through the gears and to the groans of my fellow passengers, rolled to a stop opposite them. I wound my window down and casually rested my elbow on its lower edge. The conservation that followed went something like this.

"Hi Ladies. Good afternoon to ye all," I said slowly in my best American drawl. "My friends here and my good self apologise for disturbing your walk ladies, but could you tell us if this road will lead us into the fine hamlet of Ciren – Cester?" I deliberately stumbled over the name. "We all here are in the United States Air Force," I droned like a Texan. "And we need to get to our base out on the west coast of your wonderful and quaint country." I tipped them a lazy salute with my index finger.

The girls giggled and were at a momentary loss for words. Maybe they hadn't been called *ladies* before, especially by such a good looking American? The girls quickly gained confidence and were soon crowding around the open window. Directions were given with much finger pointing. In turn, each crouched down low to peer inside the car at these strange American aliens. We further chatted for a minute or two before I said goodbye on behalf of us all.

"Well. Thank you, ladies, for your kind assistance. We all are mighty grateful to ye all. We never knew that you English girls were so helpful and so very pretty. You girls make sure you all have a nice day now."

They giggled again. With another lazy index finger salute I eased the car into gear and pushed on the accelerator. "Bye now." I drawled whilst smiling. We drove off laughing like fools. We had probably made their day. After all, how often do British teenage girls meet American fighter pilots eh?

THE END

Did you know…

Bentwaters became operational as a Royal Air Force base in 1944 during World War Two. In 1951, however, it was turned over to the United States Air Force as part of NATO's Cold War strategy. Improvements were made to bring the base up to modern NATO standards and over the years, many different types of aircraft operated from there. At the time of our visit Bentwaters was operating McDonnell Douglas F-4 Phantoms, which, from an aesthetic point of view, have always been my favourite military aircraft. They look aggressive and seem to be saying "*Don't mess with me.*"

Due to the collapse of The Berlin Wall and of The Soviet Union itself, the United States decided to pull much of its military assets out of Europe. As such, Bentwaters was handed back in 1993 to The Ministry of Defence who decided to close the base that same year. At the time of writing it is a business park and TV/film location. A museum dedicated to the base's Cold War history is located in the old command bunker.

In 1980, Bentwaters found fame when several airmen claimed to have seen a UFO in a forest very near to the base. Several books and documentaries have been written and made about the incident, and the locality still attracts UFO enthusiasts to this day.

*****

The trip to Bentwaters was certainly an adventure. It was the 1970's and way back then the journey, well in excess of two hundred miles, would be considered a long one. The new M4 motorway (From South West Wales to London) was still under construction in many places and, as such, much of the route would have been on A class roads.

*****

A 4.10 is a type of small shotgun and ideal for a beginner. I had used one myself many times. Single barrelled, light and easy to carry, it is an ideal shotgun for the young, aspiring shooter.

*****

Cirencester is a Roman town and was known as Corinium. A Roman fort was established there soon after the Roman conquest of Britain. The main settlement was the hill fort at Bagendon. Three major Roman roads met at Corinium, namely The Fosse Way, Akeman Street and Ermin Street.

THE BIG BANG

In my story entitled *Feet of Flames*, I introduced the reader to the magical substance called Carbide. Its proper name is Calcium Carbide and when I discovered it as a young teenager, I thought it the best substance on the planet. When Carbide is in contact with moisture, it gives off Acetylene gas which, as you probably do know, is a very flammable and explosive gas. Back when I was a young boy, Carbide could be freely bought from any ironmonger shop. These days it is classed as a hazardous substance and its sale is heavily restricted.

Over time, my confidence with Carbide grew as well as my complacency. Soon I was chasing after bigger and better explosions. In order to impress my science teacher with my new found knowledge, I even took a bag of the stuff into school. In all fairness to him, Mr. King took a very small quantity and used it in our next science lesson. He gathered my peers and myself around one of the large, wooden work benches and dropped the carbide into a small tin which contained water. My fellow classmates were amazed to see the water bubble and boil and most took a jump backwards as a lighted match was dropped into the mix. There was a slight pop and a few feeble flames sparked and died... 'very unimpressive' I thought considering the effects that I was used to in *my* experiments.

Considering that Mr. King had used very little Carbide, I was left with nearly a full bag of the stuff. At break time some of my classmates wanted another demonstration. They also wanted to see a bigger and better explosion. I was more than happy to oblige them.

First things first. We needed a quantity of water to drop the carbide into. We sloped off to a quiet corner of the playground, or *yard* as we called it, in order to weigh up our options. We considered filling one of the sinks in the toilets but I decided against that. From earlier experiments I envisaged a blackened and sooty stain pasted up the wall and across the ceiling. The toilets themselves were also ruled out for a similar reason.

"How about using the drains?" someone said.

"Good idea," I replied. "Let's go and have a look." The drains ran along the yard along the bottom of the external wall of the school buildings. Finding a suitable specimen, I dropped to my knees beside its metal cover and peered through the slots into the blackness below. It was too dark to see any water but I could hear it flowing through the system at a fair pace.

"This will do," I said. "There is a good quantity of water here."

With the lads keeping an eye out for wandering pupils or, even worse, a teacher, I emptied the rest of the bag of Carbide into the void below. It took some time to force the larger lumps through the slots but eventually the entire bag's contents had vanished. I could clearly hear the sibilant hiss as the carbide reacted with the water and I got back on my feet with an air of satisfaction. One of my fellow conspirators handed me a box of matches. I slid the box open and stepped forward to the drain. I could hear the water bubbling violently as I took out several matches at once.

"Stand back," I said as I ran the small bunch of matches along the striking edge of their box. They immediately burst into a yellow, bright hot-bed of flame. I took a further tentative step forward before flinging the burning mass towards the drain. Retreating quickly, I expected to hear a loud *thwomp* as the gas exploded. Instead, there was an almighty bang which reverberated around the school buildings like a twenty-one-gun salute. A sheet of hot, yellow flame shot skywards and peaked at about half way up one of the windows of the woodwork room. At the same instant, a second metal drain cover, some distance from the first, blew clean up into the air. It did a slow somersault before gravity caught hold of it and drew it back to earth.

Alongside this flying drain cover a flatbed truck was parked. Lying on the flatbed were several large panes of expensive thick glass which were part of a new chicken shed which the school was having built.... Yes. We kept chickens as part of our Rural Studies curriculum. You've already guessed what happened next haven't you? Yes. It all seemed to occur in slow motion. Gawping up at the spiraling drain cover, we all knew what was about to happen but hoping against all hope that it wouldn't. The heavy, metal cover curved back towards earth and landed smack dead centre on the glass. With a loud explosive report sounding like a pistol shot, a crack snapped through each pane rendering each one useless.

"Bloody Hell," someone exclaimed with a sharp intake of breath.

At this point, each of us did a good imitation of Roger Bannister (First person to run a mile in under four minutes) as we all disappeared around the back of the school. Finding a quiet spot away from everyone else, we quietly panicked as we searched for a suitable alibi. Just then, the shrill rattle of the school bell signaled that break time was over. The sound pierced our gloom and, glad of the distraction, we shuffled off to our next class.

It wasn't until the following morning that investigations started. To make matters worse, we had a Rural Science lesson just before lunch. Our teacher seemed upset. We all filed into class and I remember trying to look as nonchalant and innocent as possible. We all sat at our desks and awaited the start of the lesson. Mr. Mainwaring, our teacher, had lost his usual welcoming smile and explained to us in stern tones what had happened to the glass. He then asked if any of us knew anything about it? His question was answered with a tense silence; his eyes roaming around the rows of unsmiling faces in front of him. My brow flushed hot and a nausea swept through my stomach as I could sense doom approaching.

Sure enough, the dreaded call came that afternoon. I think that I was in the middle of a history lesson when a prefect knocked the door and entered. She handed a scrap of paper to Miss. Davies (Or Battle-axe as we called her). A silence shrouded the room as her eyes quickly scanned the note. Her eyes lifted and settled on me.

"Peter," she said. "The Headmaster wants to see you now."

I shuffled off with the prefect, careful not to make eye contact with anyone else. We both slowly walked the corridor not saying a word. Eventually, the prefect headed off to her class.

"Good luck," she whispered.

How my jelly like legs got me to the headmaster's office I do not know. Steeling myself, I knocked on the door.

"Come in," A sharp, business-like voice answered.

I stood erect in front of Mr. John's desk with my hands firmly locked together behind my back.

Mr. John stopped whatever he was doing and leant forward on his elbows. He then rested his chin on top of his clasped hands and just stared at me hawk like.

"Peter?" he eventually questioned. "Do you have any idea why I have sent for you?"

"No sir," I immediately replied. Thinking back, this was technically a truthful answer. He broke contact with his desk and leant back in his chair.

"As you are aware Peter, several panes of very expensive glass were broken yesterday. This was caused by some sort of explosion in the drains which made one of the heavy, metal, drain covers to fly up into the air and land on the glass." He paused before continuing. "Yesterday you showed Mr. King some Carbide, didn't you?"

"Yes Sir."

"Not long after that lesson and during break time, the explosion that smashed the glass happened." He paused again. "Now," he reasoned. "I know that I am not Sherlock Holmes, but what do you think I should determine from those facts?"

I just stood there and shrugged my shoulders. Mr. John leant forward on his elbows again. "Did you cause this explosion?" he asked quietly.

I hesitated for a second. After all, I did not want to gain a reputation for being a liar. There was also the fact to be considered that my maternal aunt was the full-time head cook at the school and that my mother often helped her out when shorthanded.

"Yes Sir," I confessed timidly as I shuffled my feet.

"I see." Mr. John replied. "Was there anyone else involved?"

I hesitated again, thinking of the repercussions if I dobbed the others in. I soon squealed like a pig though and quickly rattled off the names of the other three involved. They soon joined me, the four of us standing in a straight line before Mr. John. As we stood in silent fear, we were subjected to a lecture about responsibility, the dangers of meddling with carbide, respect for school property, the reputation of the school... not to mention the destruction of valuable glass and the delay it would cause in the construction of the new chicken shed.

The four of us left his office in guilty submission, each of us blowing on our hands. We had been on the receiving end of two raps on the palm of each hand with a vicious looking cane. We skulked off back to class with Mr. John's favourite saying ringing in our ears.

"Thank God there are good boys and girls in this school."

THE END

Did you know...

In 1954, Roger Bannister was the first person to run a mile in under four minutes after many athletes had tried to do so prior to this date. Aged 25, he achieved this in three minutes, fifty-nine point four seconds (3:59.4). In the 67 years since, the mile record has been reduced by almost 17 seconds and, at the time of writing, stands at 3:43.13. This time was run by Hicham El Guerrouj of Morocco, at age of 24, in 1999.

Running a mile in four minutes equates to a speed of 15 miles per hour.

DEL BOY

I can't remember if I ever knew Del's proper name. He was always known as just Del. He was a pleasant enough lad who was a year or two younger than myself. The both of us were at school at the same time but being younger he would, of course, have been in a lower year class. I used to see him about at school but, hard as I might try, I can't remember his face. I do remember though that he had a mop of dark, tangled hair. All I can recall with certainty is his name, Del, and the fact that he came from the top end of the village. This part of Penclawdd back then was considered bandit country and might well have been a different country to where us lowlanders lived. The youngsters that inhabited this high ground were generally considered as *the enemy.*

High up at the top end of my home village and very close to the afore mentioned *bandit country* was what one could have called back then, the municipal rubbish tip… the forerunner of the modern recycling centre. To us locals, it was simply known as *The Dump.* In my story *Feeling The Heat,* I write in some length about the dump. It was located on the site of a long-abandoned coal mine and was a popular playground to many of us adventurous lads. Here, the dust carts as we called them, would deposit all the rubbish they had collected from neighbouring households and the like.

I am writing here of a time before the concepts of *recycling* and *saving the planet* had even been thought of. There were no black rubbish bags, nor were there any blue, green or pink ones either. All we had back then was the metal rubbish bin into which everything went and which was emptied by the council once every week…. Yes. That's right…*every* week!

Anything that could not be fitted into the bin you took to the rubbish tip yourself. For those of us who had air rifles, this vast area of rubbish was what one might term a 'target rich environment'. Bottles. cans, toys, old television sets, long dead vehicles all suffered the onslaught of lead in the form of air gun pellets. I bet if it were possible today for one to sieve through the soil where the dump once was, one would find a small fortune in lead. Del lived not very far from this large pile of rubbish and, apart from seeing him at school, my only recollections of him are of when we accidentally met amongst this vast area of garbage. This story involves two separate incidents that involved him and which happened at the dump.

My brother and I would visit the dump on a fairly regular basis with his air rifle. Sometimes we would borrow a second rifle from one of his mates so that we had one each to play around with. My brother and I were mucking about on the top of an old coal tip which was rich with rubbish. The council dust carts would drive onto this tip and deposit their contents over its edges. As a consequence, the tip's top surface was flat, hard and solid; packed tight with ash from countless long dead coal fires.

We were shooting at this and that when Del suddenly appeared on an old bike that he had found amongst all the debris. He came barrelling down the dirt road towards the tip shouting with pure glee. The bike had long lost its drive chain and, as we discovered later, had no brakes. It was basically a rusty old frame with two wheels, each missing its rubber tyre. Del was riding it on its metal rims…a bumpy ride indeed.

He whizzed past us far too close for comfort. Del circled us before his momentum faded away and he was forced to stop. Laughing, he pushed his battered bike back up the hill and took up position for a second run at us.

"We'll get him this time," my brother said smugly as he picked up a long piece of metal piping which just happened to be lying around. "Just watch this."

As Del shot past us for the second time, my brother threw the length of pipe like a spear. He aimed for the back wheel and found his target spot on. The pipe ripped out the wheel's spokes one by one and the wheel collapsed in on itself. Now, as you are probably aware, bicycles do not work too well with only one wheel. Del soon discovered this as his chariot fell apart about him. It came to a violent stop, propelling him over the handlebars.

He landed on his backside with a thump, his thrashing legs scattering a heap of rubbish far and wide. Fortunately, he was none the worse for wear and nice kid as he was, saw the funny side of things. "You bastards," he shouted as he walked away grinning; rubbing both his buttocks quite tenderly as he did so. I saw him in school a few days later and he looked to be alright. Those classroom wooden chairs were quite hard though...ouch!

*****

Another adventure involving Del again took place up at the dump. As usual my brother and I were up there with his air rifle shooting at any old piece of rubbish that we considered an attractive target. We were enjoying ourselves when we heard voices coming from over the edge of an old coal tip near to where we were. We both slinked (That's not a word that I have used often!) over to the edge and looked down.

Below us was a fairly large area of flat concrete which, long ago, had been part of the colliery workings. It was the roof of some kind of building, though not much of the vertical walls were visible to the gradual pile up of rubbish. It just looked like a large raft of concrete. There were several square holes in this surface which, as we knew from previous explorations, gave access to narrow tunnels below which ran the length of the building. What this structure would have been used for I do not know but it was unusual enough, especially with its tunnels, to attract adventurous lads.

The voices belonged to Del and one of his *uplander* mates. Neither was aware that they were being spied upon from above. Del had a catapult or sling shot with him and both lads were using it to shoot small stones at a line of bottles they had set up. Their ignorance of our presence soon ended when a bottle exploded on the concrete just in front of them. I had lobbed it from above. In the few seconds of their shocked immobility, my brother shot out one of their target bottles. Recovering their wits, Del and his mate started shouting the usual expletives which, in a basic sense, translated into "Go away you boys with unmarried parents."

Such foul language was met with a second and third bottle being shot out as well as a torrent of bottles raining down around them. Glass flew in all directions like shrapnel; causing both lads to dance about trying to avoid it. The location of the concrete slab made an easy escape difficult, so both lads took the only option open to them. They dropped down into the tunnels beneath them.

Now they were really pinned down but safe from attack from bottles and lead pellets. I kept up the bottle artillery though and scored several direct hits as bottles disappeared into the tunnel to smash inside.

"Wait here," my brother ordered as he handed me the rifle. "We'll smoke them out."

Carefully, he made his way down towards the concrete slab collecting several large cardboard boxes on the way. Reaching the concrete, the boxes were flattened out by stamping on them. He then set light to some paper and dropped it into one of the holes. This was repeated at each of the other apertures. Knowing that the tunnels themselves were full of combustible rubbish, the idea was to burn or smoke the enemy out. To give extra encouragement for the smoke to build up underground, the cardboard was used to cover the holes. Having completed his task, my brother returned to our elevated vantage point.

It didn't take long for one of the pieces of cardboard to bob up with a head below it. It was Dell. As he popped up in search of air, a bottle exploded not far in front of his position. Del started screaming and clutched his face trying to stem the blood that seeped through his fingers. It took a few seconds for him to realise that the bottle had contained tomato ketchup sauce and that the blood was no more than a tasty relish.

"Surrender," my brother shouted down. "Surrender and we will let you go." Del waved his arms in capitulation as the flames below him really took hold.

Both he and his mate emerged from their tunnels with their arms raised. It looked like a scene from a World War Two film where an enemy machine gun post had been defeated. Both lads sloped off home without a word, Del still wiping tomato sauce from his hair. My brother and I also turned for home, both of us laughing and feeling very, very much the victors. A battle fought and won.

THE END

Did you know...

A Catapult is a device used to launch a projectile, such as a small stone, a great distance without the use of gunpowder or other propellants. It uses the sudden release of stored energy to propel the projectile. In use since ancient times, the catapult has been one of the most effective weapons of war, ranging from simple hand-held devices to mechanisms for launching aircraft from the deck of an aircraft carrier.

The hand-held type we used as boys we made ourselves. It consisted of a 'Y' shaped stick with a single length of elastic cord, or 'dummy elastic' as it was known, tied to the top of the two forks of the 'Y'. The elastic was threaded through the tongue of an old shoe in which the projectile was placed.

Energy was applied to the device by pulling back the elastic slowly as far as one dared, very similar to the way one would use a bow and arrow, which, incidentally, is another form of catapult. With practice, the projectile could be sent a hundred feet or more and with a fair degree of accuracy.

SECOND PLACE

The year Immediately following my discharge from the Royal Air Force I trained to be a technical teacher. I attended Dudley college in the West Midlands and completed a one-year, full time course which led to The Certificate in Education (Further Education). This qualification entitles me to teach in the secondary education sector and above. In order to do the course, one had to be over twenty-five years of age and be qualified in engineering. As such, there was no instruction in engineering itself as it was assumed that one already knew all that stuff. The main thrust was on lesson planning and a heck of a lot of teaching practice which I did at Wolverhampton Technical College. For light relief we also studied the 'ology's" ... psychology, philosophy and sociology... subjects which were alien to us pragmatic engineering grunts but were very interesting all the same.

The course was not that difficult and during the times that one was not on teaching practice, there was plenty of time available to socialise and enjoy some of the extra curricula activities on offer. A fellow student, whom, for the sake of this story I shall call Simon, was very much into cross country running. Learning that I had done some long distance running in the Royal Air Force, Simon persuaded me to join the college's cross-country running club.

I must admit here and now that I have never been able to describe myself as athletic. I hated 'gym' at school and presented many a forged letter to the Physical Education (P.E.) teacher excusing me from, what I considered to be, dangerous, pointless and sweat laden activities. My reluctance to engage in P.E. was due to a complete lack of interest combined with a total lack of talent. I was useless at Rugby, Cricket, Soccer and all other games. Despite being well over six foot two inches tall, I couldn't sprint, jump, skip, throw a javelin or discus and deservedly was always one of the last to be picked to join a particular team.

In the gymnasium my performance was even worse. I could not vault a horse; do press ups or chin ups and no way could I climb a rope. The one thing I could do though was run long races. I could plod along for hours over all sorts of outdoor terrain, enjoying the solitude and finish in a respectable time.

My first and last race with the Dudley college team was an away event somewhere further up north. Following a mini bus ride of a couple of hours we arrived at the venue. The race was to consist of a six-mile run; made up of three laps of two miles each. We were briefed on the course which, as far as I can remember, was over mud sodden fields, knee deep streams, public roads, slimy coal waste tips and public footpaths. There were well over a hundred participants and many well-known and famous running clubs were represented.

The star of the show and who totally eclipsed everyone else present, was a person who was already an Olympic and Commonwealth Games medallist. I won't mention the name as I can't be asked to find out how to ask this person's permission to do so! For the sake of the story though, I will call this famous star athlete Biff.

It was winter and the low arced sun cast a dirty white sheen over the frosted industrial landscape. We all stood around in a loose pack. Some of us were running or jumping on the spot trying to keep warm as the air rippled with feathery plumes as it met warm breath. Some runners were wearing gloves. No one had told me to bring gloves. I fumed as feeling began to drain from my quickly numbing fingers.

At last an official picked up a megaphone and told us all to get ready. The keen runners took up poses as if they were already running but frozen in time. I, and many others just shuffled forward. The whistle sounded and we were off.

As one giant pack we ran down a gently sloping field towards a shallow river. The water foamed as a hundred or so pairs of feet splashed into it. It was about ankle deep. The far bank was steep and slimy; requiring us all to scrabble up on our hands and knees. Within four of five minutes from the start, we were already wet and mottled with clinging mud. A race marshal directed us left along a narrow footpath which opened up onto a rough lane fashioned from compacted cinder.

Here, another marshal turned us right onto a tar macadamed road which gently climbed towards the seemingly far horizon. On this climb the pack of runners begin to spread out. By the time we reached the top of the hill each of us had got into our natural rhythms and pace. I remember we had to circumnavigate a large wooded park, the frost covered leaves and grass underfoot beginning to yield to the tepid warmth of the sun. We climbed two volcanic looking long abandoned coal spoil heaps, jumped a narrow stream, crossed a few more muddy fields before joining a proper road again.

I was delighted to find that I was actually passing people along the way. Those evenings spent jogging around the college playing fields seemed to be paying off. I looked with distain at those runners who were struggling. Running bent over with hands on hips and on the verge of vomiting is never a good look I thought. I reached the bottom of a long narrow street where yet another bobble hatted and woolly gloved marshal turned me right.

I was back on the original narrow footpath that paralleled the river. The river was on my left and in the far distance I could see all the buses parked up; patiently waiting to whisk us all away to our various warm and comfortable abodes. To my right there was a long distressed looking wall which bordered the neglected back gardens of red bricked terraced houses. The buildings looked as if they had been there for ever, defying both time and the harsh elements.

The further I ran the more I could hear distant cheering coming from somewhere ahead. In the distance I could see a lone runner. As I closed on him, I recognised him as Biff, the star runner. Digging my heels in hard, I called upon my diminishing reserve of energy. I was really in my stride and sensed that I was doing well. I caught up with Biff and was so close to him that the toes of my running shoes were almost clipping the back of his. I tried to overtake him but the narrow footpath prevented me doing so. He looked over his shoulder and took a fleeting glance at me. Biff upped his pace but I remained stuck to his heels.

Up ahead the shouting and cheering had become intense as the race supporters took in this two-person race fast approaching them. Two marshals held the finishing tape across the width of the cinder lane. Who would get there first everyone wondered? Biff and I upped our game and approached the finish at a sprint. As expected, he broke the tape and came to a panting stop amongst his admiring fans.

I ran past him and gave a cheery and cheeky wave to the Dudley supporters. They watched as if frozen in time. Open mouthed and with their gloved hands motionless in mid applause, their enthusiasm collapsed as I sailed past them. The marshal was still standing there on that first corner grinning. He directed me, yet again, towards that long sloping hill that signalled the start of my *third* lap… Biff finished first. I eventually finished in sixty seventh position. Not a bad effort I thought.

THE END

Did you know…

Cross country running comes under the umbrella sport of athletics and is a natural terrain version of long-distance track and road running. The courses for such races can take participants over fields, through woodland, over hills, across open country, through rivers and streams and along footpaths as well as open country road. Such races are usually held in autumn and winter and, as such, can involve rain, sleet, snow, hail and a wide range of temperatures.

Although open air running competitions are ancient, the rules and traditions of the sport originated in Britain. The first national competition was the English Championship which was run in 1876. The first International Cross-Country Championships was held in 1903 and since 1973, the foremost competition for elite runners has been the World Athletic Cross-Country Championships.

THINGS AIN'T ALWAYS WHAT THEY SEEM

Elsewhere in this collection of stories I have mentioned the fact that the village of Penclawdd, where my brother and I were raised overlooks a vast tidal estuary. The locals refer to this area as *The Marsh*. This area is characterised by raised mud banks; topped with flat green carpets of salt resistant turf and spiky spartina cordgrass.

Running east/west, *The Marsh* has its northern and southern edges guarded by two tidal rivers. These rivers make access difficult which usually involves wading through slimy mud and fast flowing tidal water. Adding to these problems, the whole area is punctuated by long meandering rivers which have been carved out of the mud by the ebb and flow of timeless tides. These are known as *pills* which vary dramatically in terms of length, width and depth. These really are a maze and unless one is familiar with the area, they can really hinder the progress of the wild fowler or fisherman and the like. One has to keep an eye on the tides and the amount of water running in the tidal river that parallels the shoreline of the village. My brother and his mates from the shooting and fishing fraternity were no exception for the need to carefully scrutinise the tides.

One such mate whom I shall call Lewis, came up with an idea that would make access to the marshes much easier…to build a boat. He produced plans for a simple punt and, following discussions with my brother, the decision was made to build it. Marine ply wood was bought and the project was entered into with great enthusiasm.

Permission was sought and granted by a local market gardener to construct the punt in one of his large greenhouses. The build went well and a fine craft resulted. The project planning could have been a bit better though for when the punt was finished, it was discovered that it was too large to fit through the door of the greenhouse. With cap in hand, my brother and Lewis had to seek permission to remove one of the larger windows in order to extricate their creation.

The punt was moored on the landward side of the tidal river until needed. This made it readily accessible and relatively easier to cross over to the marshes without worrying too much about the state of the tides. Once safely across, the punt was secured by anchor and progress then made by foot. Sometimes though, depending on the tides, the occupants remained in the punt which was allowed to gently drift along some of the wider and longer pills. Crouching low and with shotguns ready, they patiently waited for any wayward duck to fly within shooting range. I remember doing this a few times with my brother; probably imagining that I was in the upper reaches of the Amazon or somewhere equally exotic.

One winter though and following a bad storm combined with a high tide, the punt vanished. Following a search, the craft was spotted about a mile or so upriver. It was sitting on a grass topped mud bank the marsh side of the river. It looked fine and none the worse for its adventure. A day or two later my brother and Lewis decided to recover the punt after a few hours of duck shooting.

Time marched on. The tide turned and began to flow back up the estuary. Knowing the punt was available and waiting, neither shooter was worried too much about the river filling up. Eventually though they decided to call it a day and weaving around the maze of now rapidly filling pills, they headed for the waiting craft.

The punt was sitting near the river bank. The plan was to launch it and row down river against the incoming tide to a spot near to where it was usually kept. As we all know though, the best laid plans often go awry. Approaching the punt it looked in good order. Upon reaching it though, both lads were horrified at the sight that greeted them.

The far side of the punt…the side that could not be seen from shore or from their line of approach, was lying flat on the grass. The four-sided punt now only had three sides! It was also observed that the grass surrounding the punt had been churned up by the horses that lived on the marsh. Apparently, the horses had started to use the punt as a scratching post; something that it was not designed for. The structure eventually surrendered to the pressures caused by the scratching and had given way. The punt lay there in a state of rigor mortis. No better than a pile of firewood.

A quick look at the river confirmed my brother's and Lewis's worst fears. The cold, black water was too deep to wade across and was getting deeper by the second. There was only one thing for it. A mad dash up the estuary! Like Superman, leaping over water filled pills with a single bound; slipping and sliding on the mud underfoot, they raced against the incoming tide. Out of breath and sweating heavily from exertion and fear, they both eventually reached a point way up the estuary where the water was not too deep. They carefully waded across this unfamiliar part of the river and gratefully put foot on shoreside terra firma.

I don't know what happened to the punt. My brother tells me that it was eventually recovered and I do have a vague memory of it sitting in our back garden for some time afterwards. I have no idea whether or not attempts were made to repair it. One thing I do know though. It never floated again.

THE END

Did you know…
A punt is a flat-bottomed boat with a square cut bow and stern, thus making them basically rectangular in shape. They are propelled by pushing against the river bed with a long pole or with the end of an oar. A punt has no keel and its shallow draft makes it an ideal craft for manoeuvring in shallow waters, even when fully laden. From what I have read, punts are traditionally associated with the River

Thames and were used as small cargo boats or as platforms for fishermen and wildfowlers.

The square cut bow and stern gives greater carrying capacity compared with a similar sized boat with a narrow or pointed bow. This shape also makes the punt a very stable craft and suitable for carrying both cargo as well as passengers.

A LOAD OF HOT AIR

In 1982 on more or less a whim, I emigrated to Australia. For ten years I lived and worked under its wide azure skies and can now proudly boast that I hold both Australian citizenship *and* an Australian passport. I had been there previously so I knew more or less what to expect. I also knew that most Australians loved life and had a layback attitude towards almost everything. Such an attitude became evident when I had my first job interview. I was a technical teacher and had arranged several job interviews at various Australian schools before leaving the UK.

I arrived promptly for the interviews looking very smart in shirt and tie and wearing long, perfectly ironed trousers with creases so sharp that they would have sliced through flesh with ease. The school where I eventually taught at was a Catholic one and affiliated to the Christian Brothers. The hierarchy of the school were Brothers themselves who wore blue shirts with white dog collars, including the Principal, Brother Paul.

Shortly after arriving for my interview I was ushered into his office and took the offered seat. Brother Paul was a short, well-built man who was probably in his early forties. He had well-groomed jet-black hair and a very easy and jolly way about him. He made me feel very welcome. With the casual chit chat over with, I began to explain my teaching experience. With me I had my mighty red backed ring leaf folder which contained all of my qualifications, references, testimonials and the like. Brother Paul looked at the offered folder and without even opening it, pushed it back towards me.

"I don't need to see that Peter," he said in his thick Australian accent. "All I need to know is can you bloody well teach mate? Tell you what. I'll give you a go and see how it goes eh?" He then smiled and nodded towards my attire. "And another thing Peter. Get rid of those trousers, shirt and tie. It's shorts and T-shirt here mate!" That was as formal as the interview ever got and I stayed at that school for eight fantastic years.

You may or may not know that in 1988 Australia celebrated its bicentenary. That is, two hundred years of white occupation. Two hundred years since the First Fleet of convicts sailed into what is now known as Sydney Harbour. The Federal Government, under the auspices of the legendary Labour Prime Minister Bob Hawk, decided that the nation should party. Millions of dollars were allocated to these celebrations with each of the six states getting its fair share.

The first I knew about these celebrations was when I discovered a leaflet which had been thrust into my mail box. I gave it a cursory glance and learnt that it had come from the local council, or shire offices to be exact, and was something to do with the bicentenary.

Once back indoors I examined the leaflet in detail. It explained about the nationwide celebrations and that our shire had been given a pot of money in order to celebrate this momentous year in the nation's history. Furthermore, the leaflet invited shire residents to attend a public meeting in order to put forward ideas and to discuss how this money be best spent.

The meeting was held in the Shire Hall and upon arrival I found a quiet, inconspicuous seat right at the back. A good handful of people stood up in turn and expressed their ideas. None really grabbed my interest though. None that is until a man, a few rows in front of myself, addressed the meeting. He explained that during the bicentennial year there was to be an international hot air balloon race across Australia, starting in Perth in Western Australia and ending in Sydney in New South Wales.

With deference to the year, eighty-eight balloons from around the world would be invited to take part. The race was to comprise of competitive ballooning events in various towns along the continent and would be of two weeks duration. Between events, the balloonists would drive in convoy to the next location. As well as its competitive nature, the event would also display hot air ballooning to the public at large. Many living along the route would have never experienced the spectacle of seeing even just one balloon up close, not to mention eighty-eight of them!

The man then put forward his idea. In a nutshell, he suggested that the Shire acquire a hot air balloon, train several residents to fly it and enter the race. Mild laughter sprinkled the room, but he stuck by his guns and the idea was duly noted. Being something of an adventurer, hot air ballooning was something I had always wanted to do. As the meeting concluded and people began to disperse, I approached the man in question and introduced myself. His name was Michael. He explained that he had some experience of ballooning and it was through his contacts in the sport that he had first learnt of the race.

A few weeks later we were both invited to attend the Shire Hall in order to meet Paul, the bicentenary coordinator. Paul explained that the ballooning project had been approved and that the Shire would sponsor the cost of training four residents to become qualified balloon pilots. Michael and I though, would be required to choose the other two future pilots and to find a suitable training provider. This all sounded quite positive until it was explained to us that we would also have to acquire a balloon ourselves. The budget, we were told, would not stretch that far. We both felt quite buoyed up as we left the meeting whilst asking ourselves 'How hard can it be to find a hot air balloon?'

Many letters were sent out to large corporations explaining our project and asking if they would wish to sponsor us. Many weeks went by without a bite and then, out of the blue, a letter arrived from the Mazda motor vehicle corporation. It stated that they were interested in supporting us and hoped that the enclosed cheque for twenty-five thousand dollars would help...Result! Their only stipulation was that the balloon be emblazoned with the MAZDA logo.

We ordered a brand-new balloon and had it made in the colours of the local rugby league team, The Sharks…blue and white. The word MAZDA appeared twice in giant black lettering around the balloon's circumference. The whole effect was very impressive. By this time we had found our two new prospective pilots and had persuaded the local MAZDA dealer to provide us, on a long lend arrangement, a brand-new people carrier complete with trailer to facilitate transport of crew and balloon. At last we were in business.

One Friday evening at the start of winter in 1987, the four of us headed west from Sydney on a great adventure. We were heading deep into New South Wales to a small, rural town where our pilot training was to take place. It was a four hour drive each way and we did that trip almost every weekend for many, many weeks. Our instructors were very experienced and very good. Initially, we sat for hours in a room at our hotel and were introduced to the mysteries of meteorology. navigation and balloon operations. We also learnt how to assemble our balloon and perform various safety checks before it was allowed to leave the ground. With all this information embedded in our minds, we then started our flying training.

It may still be the case but back then, in order to qualify for one's private balloon pilot's licence, one had to complete a minimum of sixteen hours as what was known as 'Pilot In Command' (PIC). One had an instructor present, but it was the trainee pilot who would actually fly the balloon.

I can't remember how far I was into my pilot training, but one bright and early morning I was the Pilot In Command with my instructor, Michael, standing behind me. We were flying at about five hundred feet altitude when I reached up to fire the gas burner which would, when required, fire off a long flame and thus heat the air inside the balloon. This hot air, which rises, would provide lift and allow the balloon to ascend. Relevant to this story is the fact that I am a tall man, long limbed with very bony elbows. Reaching for the burner my right elbow collided heavily with Michael's head. I mumbled an apology but thought nothing else of it as I continued to concentrate on my flying. A minute or so ticked by before I realised that Michael was not responding to the comments I was making.

I swivelled around and found that he was missing. For a horrendous second or two I thought that my blow had sent him overboard, but then I then noticed him sitting in the bottom of the gondola cupping his bloodied nose and moaning in pain. So, there I was, five hundred feet up in the air, a novice pilot and with my flying instructor barely conscious.

Whilst I was trying to assess Michael's condition my concentration drifted and the balloon, cooling off, began to descend. Realising that there was woodland beneath us I fired the burner. I fired it for far too long and we shot upwards like a rocket to something like seven hundred feet. The balloon was drifting towards a very large field so I decided, even though not qualified to do so, to try and land there. I needed to lose height fast so pulled the line that opened the flap at the top of the balloon, thus spilling hot air. I left it open for longer than I should have and we started to take on the flying characteristics of a house brick. We had lost so much hot air that I could actually see the balloon envelope begin to cave in.

I grabbed the burner control again and gave a long, panicked blast of flame. Gradually we stopped descending but then started going up again. This bobbing up and down continued for about ten minutes until I eventually managed to stabilize the balloon. By this time Michael, thankfully, had found his feet and recovered enough to take over control and land. Fortunately, Michael saw the funny side of the experience and quickly recovered even though he sported a black eye for several weeks. Of course, the story swept throughout the ballooning fraternity like a bush fire and for ever afterwards I was lumbered with the nickname "elbows."

*****

As an aside, the four of us did qualify as balloon pilots and we did enter the race across Australia. Of the eighty-eight balloons from all corners of the world that entered, we came a respectable forty third in the points table. Quite a good effort really.

THE END

Did you know…

I need to point out that many Aboriginal people fiercely objected to the whole idea of the bicentenary. They saw it not as a celebration but rather as an *occupation* of Australia by the white Europeans. To them, 1988 was a year of mourning. There were many protests and on January 26th (Australia Day) more than forty thousand people, including Aborigines from across the country and non-indigenous supporters, staged a march in Sydney, chanting for land rights as well as human rights. This plea for justice was successful in placing indigenous issues in the public consciousness.

*****

The only real control a hot air balloon pilot has over his or her craft is vertical movement, that is, 'up' and 'down'. To go 'up', the pilot fires a gas burner which causes a large blame to blast forth and which forces hot air into the bowels of the balloon itself. To go 'down', the pilot can either let the balloon cool down naturally, or pull on a lanyard which opens a vent at the very top of the balloon. With the vent open, the hot air escapes into the atmosphere and the balloon begins to descend. With practice, and by manipulating the burner and vent together, the pilot can control the rate of decent with accuracy.

For sideways movement, the pilot is at the sole mercy of the direction of localised air movement. If the breeze is coming from the north, then the balloon will move south. If coming from the east, the balloon will travel west and so it goes on. One trick is to climb to about one thousand feet and take note of altitudes where sideways direction changes. At 100 feet, for example, one might be moving east, but at 400 feet movement might be south. At 800 feet, movement might be east again.

As such, if one wants to move say northwards, then one descends to an altitude where the air was moving in that direction. It is not an exact science as the breezes are fickle and can play tricks with the balloon. One competitive challenge is to drop a small sandbag onto a target some distance away from the launch point. This involves finding an altitude where the air is moving in the direction of the target. One is very lucky if one's sandbag lands anywhere near the target. It is good fun trying though.

TEA FOR TWO

I have absolutely no idea what my brother and myself were doing in South Gower. We lived on the northern edge of the peninsula which, in geographical terms, was not that far away from the south but far enough for us to have a good reason for being there. The reason was probably something to do with shooting or fishing or crabbing and the like. These were, and still are, activities which my older brother, Brian, enjoys. Myself, being younger by seven years, just tended to tag along.

I think that we were heading back to my brother's car, a second-hand Ford Prefect, these days considered a *classic.* We had just left a wooded area and were trudging alongside a hedgerow which bordered a field. It must have been late in the day as I remember a watery, low sun casting long shadows across the grass. It was unfamiliar territory to us both but we knew in which general direction we needed to go. We were, in fact, trespassing and we steered a wide berth from the farmhouse which was over on our left. We were making good progress when a loud voice pierced the evening air.

"You two," the voice snapped. "Where do you think you are off to?"

We both spun around on our heels and faced a lone figure who was approaching us from behind. It was obviously the farmer who's land we were on. He was wearing mud-stained blue overalls and a knitted woollen cap sat tightly on his head. He was tall and thin and his attitude menacing. Trailing alongside him was an aged looking sheep dog. A Collie that looked as if it had seen better days. The conversation that followed went something like this.

"Who us?" my brother replied.

"Yes. You two. What are you doing here? This is my land you are trespassing on." He stepped closer and I noticed that his face was hard and pinched. He wore glasses but he looked over them as he spoke to us, adding to the visual effect of menace. Looking back to that time, I reckon he was in his early sixties.

"Oh!" my brother said. "I was hoping we would bump into you."

"Why were you hoping to bump into me?" the farmer said mockingly, emphasising the word *bump*. "Where are you both from?"

"We come from Penclawdd. This is my brother."

"Penclawdd eh! A bit far from home, aren't you?"

"Yes. I suppose we are, but we noticed that you have caravans on your property?" My brother vaguely pointed in the direction that, we indeed, had seen a small cluster of caravans.

"Yes. I have," answered the farmer. "I run a small caravan park here. What of it?"

I had no idea where this conversation was headed so I elected to remain quiet. Very quietly I slowly inched my way closer to my brother.

"Well," my brother continued. "My father has two caravans which he wants to put in this area somewhere. Do you have any room on your caravan park?"

In all of my many years on this planet, I have never seen the demeanour of any person change as fast as that of that farmer. One moment he was a menacing threat. The next it was as if he had just discovered his two lost sons.

"Why yes," he said with a friendly grin painted across his face. "There is plenty of room here. Come with me and I will show you the park and the facilities that we have here. They are not much, but we improve things as time and money allow."

As he led us back along the path we had already come, my brother caught my eye and gave a resigned shrug of his shoulders and a knowing wink. There were four caravans in all; spaced out on a large square of closely mown grass which was bordered by large boulders. At least two of the caravans were occupied. One had a line of washing drying whilst another had three deckchairs planted outside and surrounded by a haphazard array of toys. On one of the chairs the corners of a newspaper rippled quietly in the evening breeze.

We both showed great interest as the farmer showed us a toilet and shower block which had seen better days. Opposite, was a children's playground containing three battered swings and a steel climbing frame that leaned to one side. The swings quietly swayed and twisted with the prevailing airs. They creaked with rust. Moving on, we were shown the vacant sites, three concrete slabs just big enough to support a caravan each. My brother nodded his head with great enthusiasm.

"This looks fine," he said. "Lovely views looking towards the woods and only a short walk to the coast and the beaches."

"Aye," The farmer replied. "Lovely beaches around here and plenty of fresh air." He breathed in deeply and patted his chest as if to reinforce the point.

"My father will have to come and see this. It's what he is looking for, I'm sure. Can I bring him here?"

"Of course you can. Bring him anytime you want but better telephone me first just in case I'm out in the fields. Come to the house and I'll give you details. You can also meet the wife and have a cup of tea with us."

"Thank you," my brother replied. "We would both enjoy that."

On the walk to the farmhouse I trailed behind as the other two discussed rents and other money related matters. At this point I don't think I had spoken a single word. The house was large and grey with faded window frames painted green. We reached a half-glazed storm porch and our host loosened his boots against a metal boot scraper set beside the door. He kicked them off and we followed suit.

"Come on in lads and mind that high step."

Coming inside from the evening air the heat of the living room hit me like a hammer. Its source was a large wood fire which hissed and groaned as it continuously settled in the large, wrought iron grate. The flames danced red and threw deep shadows across the natural stone walls which had been painted a dull matt white. The room had a cosy glow about it and soaked with the delicious smell of wood smoke.

A large and heavy looking dining table sat solidly near the one and only window. It had a green table cloth made from some heavy material. It hung over the sides of the table and had ornate tassels hanging from its edging. I remember it because we had an identical one at home. Guarding the table were three tired looking upholstered tall backed chairs; each a little threadbare through years of use. My brother and I were directed towards them.

"Sit down boys."

As we made ourselves comfortable, our host's wife appeared.

"Hello," she said with a jolly tone to her voice. "Who might you two be then?"

She was a big woman with a kindly looking moon shaped face. A mop of curly greying blonde hair sat high atop her head. Thinking back, she was an archetypical farmer's wife. A practical woman who could put her hand to anything in the kitchen and elsewhere in the house. She was wiping her hands in her white apron. I think she intended to shake hands with us but thought better of it.

Her husband told her the story of how he had met us and the fact that our father might be interested in siting two caravans on their land. She clasped her hands in delight.

"That's wonderful news. Now then. You boys must be hungry. Yes?"

We both replied with an awkward affirmative.

Within minutes the table was covered with real china cups and saucers with matching plates adorned with all sorts of niceties. Fruit cake, Welsh cakes and jam sandwiches surrounded a large teapot. Having seen us both right, the farmer and his wife settled on their favourite chairs, one either side of the fire.

Between bites of cake and sips of tea we all chatted about this and that. The farmer asked what my father did for a living. My brother told him that he was an electronic engineer and was involved in secret government work. He also explained that dad already had three caravans on sites on North Gower. One in Llangennith and two in Llanmadoc, both popular tourist locations.

A large pendulum clock hanging above the mantlepiece patiently ticked the minutes away. Eventually, the cake and tea, as well as the conversation began to fade. After a socially acceptable time we made our excuses to leave. We shook hands with the farmer; said our goodbyes and gave our thanks to his wife for a wonderful and unexpected tea. The couple stood on the high step as we recovered our boots.

"As I said. Bring your father here anytime," the farmer repeated. He handed a sheet of paper to my brother. "That's my name and telephone number. Ring first to make sure that I will be here."

"Ok," replied my brother. "I'm sure that he will be ringing you soon."

We again gave our thanks and headed for the gate that led onto the main road. Before we disappeared from view, we turned and looked back. There they were, both still standing together and giving us a cheerful wave. We waved back and fell from their view. We both laughed like a pair of wild fools as we hurried towards the car. We couldn't believe what we had just done.

Of course, our father did not own *any* caravans. He *never* had owned any and *never* did. Neither did he work for the government. He was just an ordinary television repair man. Initiated by my brother, we had both lied through our teeth to get out of a sticky situation and a possible charge of trespass. I don't think either of us ventured to that part of South Gower again…ever!

THE END

Did you know…
'A lie is like a bald spot. The bigger it gets, the harder it becomes to cover up.'

UNDER FIRE

Directly opposite the back door of our home in Penclawdd was a substantial single-story brick building with a slate tiled gable roof. To the family, it was simply known as *The Shed*. It was subdivided by solid brick walls into three different rooms, each with its own wooden door facing towards the back garden. Each room had electric light. Furthest from the house was the outside toilet. Yes. An outside toilet...remember them?

The next compartment in the shed was probably the same size as the loo. As far as I can remember it was used to store all types of junk, but I can't remember what. Maybe it was where I kept my bike when I eventually got one? On the other hand, maybe not. Then came the main and biggest room which was my father's workshop. His occupation was that of television repair engineer but as well as doing this professionally, he also used to hobble in this role for people in the village and the surrounding area.

The room boasted a workbench and shelves stacked full of electronic parts and test instruments. There was usually a number of televisions, radios and other electronic gadgets awaiting or undergoing repair. Some were simply used for a cheap supply of spare parts. The shed had a Belfast sink and a single tap which supplied cold mains water. The internal walls had been professionally plastered, but these pink surfaces bore the usual scars of a busy workshop. It was in this room that my father did his repairs and generally pottered about.

The shed had a large window which looked out onto the back garden. It was made up of individual panes of glass. I think it was about four panes high and maybe six across...making it about twenty-four panes, each of about A4 size. Over the years four of these panes had cracked and one evening, and out of the blue, my father announced that he was going to replace them.

"I want you to remove the four damaged panes," he said to Brian, my brother. He handed him a small hammer. "You can tap them out with this but be careful you don't damage any other panes."

"OK," Brian said, as he took the offered hammer.

"Do it tomorrow when I am at work. I want to replace the glass Saturday morning. I have already bought four replacement panes." Brian nodded in compliance.

The following morning though, Brian had other ideas as how to remove the damaged glass. I have mentioned elsewhere in my collection of stories that my brother had an air rifle (See *Dodging a Bullet*). Even though it was the weakest of the airguns available back then, it could still pack a powerful punch, especially at short range. Brian grabbed the rifle from where it lived in a kitchen corner and beckoned me to follow him outside.

"We'll shoot the glass out," he said in a wicked tone.

My joy was hard to contain. This was exciting stuff as only in cowboy, gangster and war films did one get to see windows being blown to pieces in this fashion. This was for real though.

"I want you to go into the shed and lie down on the floor face downwards," Brian instructed. "You won't get hurt. The glass and pellets will be flying about well above you. You can have a go later."

I lay prostrate on the cold concrete floor. "Ready," I shouted. The first lead pellet blasted through the glass, whizzed over me and thwacked into the plastered wall opposite the window. About half a dozen more followed, showering the workbench and myself with fine shards of glass. Our mother knew what was going on but she just gave a sigh of acceptance and looked the other way.

"Ok," Brian shouted. "Your turn, Let's swap places."

I took charge of the rifle and shot out the remaining glass as he took his turn lying on the shed's floor. With no more glass left to be blasted away, this mad game ended. My brother set to work removing the small bits of glass remaining and the ancient putty that once held the panes in place.

"Oh no," he said with a note of despair in his voice. "Look at this?"

I walked over to where he was working as did our mother.

"What's the matter? she asked. My brother pointed to a fifth pane of glass. It had a ragged hole in one corner with a cobweb of cracks leading away from it. It had been hit in error.

"You bloody idiot," Brian shouted. "It's your fault. Dad will go nuts." Our mother just dropped her head in shame.

Being young, I accepted the fact that I was to blame without question. Thinking back though, there was no actual proof that the wayward pellet had been fired by myself. My brother could have equally been the culprit but, unfortunately, sixty odd years later the Statute of Limitations has run out.

As we stared at the damage, the same question instantly entered all three heads, namely, what my father would do when he found out that five panes, not four, had to be replaced? 'Do his nut,' was an apt answer to that question. My brother delicately removed the fifth pane. This time though, he did the job properly and without the use of the air rifle. Five rectangular empty spaces stared back at us.

The both of us, with the collusion of our mother, hurriedly concocted a story which would appease my father's temper and place no blame on any of his wayward offspring. The story was that the fifth pane must have had a fine crack in it which had got worse due to the vibrations caused by gently tapping out the other panes.

As expected, our father 'blew his top' when he was told what had happened. He ranted and raged at the fact that he now had to go back to the glazier and order an additional pane. To the great relief of all concerned though, he bought our story hook, line and sinker. As with many other acts of mischief performed by his two offspring, he went to his grave never knowing the truth about that day.

THE END

Did you know…

The village of Penclawdd where I was raised didn't get a sewage system until the late 1950's or even later depending where one lived. The outside loo was the norm in the village and elsewhere.

Ours was about three-foot-wide and extended the whole width of *the shed* which was about six feet. At the far end and opposite the door was a wooden bench type seat which spanned the entire width of the loo. This was the business end…the Drop Box as it was sometimes known. The wooden seat was supported on a short brick wall built high enough to allow one to sit in relative comfort. In the centre of this wooden bench was a hole on which one sat to do one's business. Underneath was a bucket which could be accessed by lifting the seat which was hinged. The walls were white washed and, for sanitation purposes, handfuls of white lime powder would be thrown into the bucket after use.

Once a week the council sewage lorry would arrive. Us lads called this the *shit lorry*. A workman would collect the bucket and with practiced ease, deposit its contents into the back of the covered truck. He would then return the bucket to its rightful place ready for the next load to build up over the following week. What a job eh?

HANGING BY A THREAD

I joined the Royal Air Force in the winter of 1971. On January 25th to be precise. That was the day I, and others like me, took the oath of allegiance to Her Majesty The Queen at the local RAF recruitment office. From that point on, mum and dad did not own me. The RAF did!

A short time later I started my journey towards my newly chosen life and career. Fronting up at Swansea railway station I walked along the platform towards the train that would take me into the unknown. I walked alongside the carriages looking for a compartment to settle into. Back then there were no 'open plan' railway carriages. Each had separate compartments, connected by a side corridor.

I had almost reached the halfway point of the train when I saw several figures beckoning me from within. They were some of the other lads whom had taken the oath with me. Throwing my new suitcase onto the overhead shelf, I settled in to their greetings. I was glad that I had found company. It was to be a long journey and, besides, there is safety in numbers.

We were all heading for Royal Air Force Swinderby in Lincolnshire. It was where we were to receive our introduction into service life before being moved onto our various trade training units. Six weeks of what was called "Square Bashing", which refers to learning how to march and other things. I cannot remember how long the train journey took or where the route took us, but at some time that afternoon we were duly deposited on the platform at Newark railway station. Our joining instructions had told us to wait there until a coach arrived to collect us. From the station we would be transported to RAF Swinderby.

Along the way, more and more young recruits joined the train having connected from various far-flung corners of the land. By the time the train pulled away from Newark there was a fair crowd of us standing about waiting. Some were very quiet, but most of us were full of boisterous bravado, pretending that we were not scared or nervous as to what lay ahead. Pretending that we were real men I suppose.

Eventually a dark blue RAF coach arrived. Apart from the driver the only other person aboard was an RAF Regiment corporal. He greeted us all with a cheery smile.

"Good afternoon gentlemen," he said politely in a thick, Irish accent. "If you would be so kind as to deposit your suit cases and bags in the storage compartment and then take a seat, we will transport you to Swinderby."

He seemed very jolly and a nice chap. He boarded the coach last and sat next to the driver. As we pulled away from the station the vociferous conversations were long dead. We all sat in silence, each locked in his own thoughts. The only sound was the struggling engine and the crashing of gears as the old coach picked up speed.

I rested my weary head against the cold window and watched rivulets of rain water slowly trace their random paths along the glass. 'What on earth have I done?' I thought. 'Have I made a mistake?' In my mind's eye I pictured my warm bed back home and all the other home comforts that I had left behind. It was too late now though. The RAF owned me and I was at its mercy. There was no turning back.

RAF Swinderby appeared in the far distance looking like all other RAF stations, functional and efficient. Only the lofty water tower broke the long horizon of flat rooftops. The station's playing fields glided past and soon the driver geared down as we approached the main gate. The coach stopped outside a large, two storey building which had a pair of impressive wooden doors. The corporal stood up and faced us all.

"Right you lot. You are in the RAF now. Wake up and move your arses off this bus," he bellowed. "Grab your cases and line up outside. And cut the chatter." So much for mister nice guy I thought.

"Follow me," he ordered. Picking up our cases we did as he bid. He led us into a ground floor dormitory containing twenty-two beds, each with a mattress. Next to each bed stood a tall, narrow wooden locker accompanied by a matching bedside cabinet. In these, all our worldly goods would be kept. In the middle of the room stood a lonely looking wooden table and two chairs. The table had seen better days.

"Find a bed and sit on it and do it NOW." We fumbled in confusion, bumping into each other until we sorted ourselves out. As we all sat in silence the corporal disappeared, only to be immediately replaced by a much taller figure with three stripes on his arm. He stood in the doorway and patiently observed us with a face like granite. He wore a cap with a very steeply angled, highly polished visor which forced his head backwards in order to see. His hands were clasped behind his back. He looked impressive.

"Get your notebooks and pens out," he barked. Stepping forward into the room he revealed a clipboard containing several sheets of official looking paper. "From now on, you lot will be forever known as Twelve Flight. Now write that down." He then called out our names in turn and gave each of us our brand-new service number. During the next twenty minutes various gems of information were thrown at us. Each was eagerly written down.

"By the way," he finally said with a hint of menace. "My name is Sergeant Melville. No need to write that down because you will never forget it." He was right. I never have forgotten it.

The remainder of that day was spent collecting uniform, bedding and other odds and ends from the clothing store. The day ended with the obligatory haircut, whether or not one needed one. When I reported for my hair cut there must have been two dozen other lads in front of me in the queue. I sat down to a long wait. I was out of there within twenty minutes, complete with a very short 'back and sides.' As each victim sat in the barber's chair he was asked "How would you like it?" No matter what the reply was, each recruit was given an identical haircut, each only being in the chair for only a few minutes as the electric clippers did their cruel work. The barber charged two shillings (10 new pence) a pop. He must have made a fortune.

So there we were. Twenty-two lads all thrown together in the name of 'Queen and Country'. Twenty-two total strangers from all over the country. Different backgrounds. Different accents and different experiences and attitudes. Brothers in arms. We spent our 'square bashing' six weeks learning how to march. How to iron shirts and press trousers. How to march. How to polish shoes and boots to a mirror finish. How to dust. How to sweep floors. How to march. We learnt how to clean toilets and shower blocks. How to salute officers. How to march. We learnt to shoot a real rifle. How to kill a straw filled sack with a bayonet and how to march. In the classroom we learnt RAF History. Learnt how to identify different ranks. Learnt aircraft recognition and probably many other things that I have long forgotten.

We did cross country runs. Attacked assault courses. Crawled through water filled pipes. Got covered in mud and learnt how to march. We even learnt how to build improvised shelters in a frost-bitten Sherwood Forest and lived there for days, half freezing to death. One thing we also learnt about was the new decimal currency that was introduced on 15th February of that year, 1971. We had formal lessons about it and shown each of the new coins. I was not impressed and much preferred the old pennies, three penny bits, six penny pieces, two-shilling pieces and half crowns. When you held half a crown in your hand you knew you had some real money. This new lightweight stuff felt like rubbish.

In the gymnasium we learnt how to climb a rope. Do push ups and pull ups. How to vault a wooden horse and run around in endless circuits. Oh! Did I tell you? We also learnt how to march. In fact, whenever we moved around RAF Swinderby during working hours, we were not allowed to walk or run. We had to march as a flight of airmen with one of us taking command. This gave each of us a chance to bellow out orders, "By the leeeeft. Quick March. Leeeeft turn. About turn. Halt!". All good fun really.

Very quickly we changed from twenty-two individuals and morphed into a team. This is what the RAF wanted and expected. We helped each other and used each individual's talents to the advantage of us all. As time progressed, all twenty-two of us got to know each other reasonably well. After all, we did everything together and even shared the same bedroom. On day one of our training we were all complete strangers and a bit wary of each other. By week six we would have laid down our lives for each other. We were Twelve Flight after all and we were damned proud of that fact.

There was one chap amongst us though who stood out as being a bit odd. A lad whom none of us liked very much. His name was Brown. He was a bit of a whinger and never really tried to be part of the team in any meaningful way. He was also a bit of a stranger to soap and water and stank a bit, a characteristic for which he became infamous. As the weeks progressed and our antipathy towards Brown increased, he got the blame from the rest of us for everything that went wrong. If our dormitory failed an inspection then Brown got the blame. If our marching was not up to scratch, Brown got the blame. Thinking about it, we simply used him to vent our frustrations for things which, really, were the fault of us all.

His lack of personal hygiene reached a point where it became a standing joke. We voiced our concerns to him several times but he just laughed them off. One evening we all hatched a plan that might get our point across to him. We would put him on trial, the charge being 'Failure to maintain proper standards of hygiene in Her Majesty's Royal Air Force' or something like that. A trumped-up summons was typed up in the station library which included the date and time that Brown was to appear in court. This document was sealed in an envelope and left on his bed where he was certain to find it.

On the evening of the trial we used several beds to fashion a courtroom, The table doubled as the Judge's bench and a single chair formed 'The Dock'. The second chair was the witness stand. We then drew our respective make-believe parts from a hat. Judge, Jury, Prosecution and Defence Counsel, Witnesses, Clerk to the Court and Police Officer. Brown lay on his bed watching somewhat apprehensively as the courtroom took shape. Purely by chance, I drew the part of the Judge and wore a wig carefully crafted from newspaper. When all was ready, I drew the court to order by rapping a tin mug on the table top. The trial began and went something like this:

The Police Officer escorted Brown to "The Dock". In all fairness to Brown, he could have just lain on his bed or even left. He played along though, somewhat reluctantly. The Clerk to the Court took command of the room.

"Hear ye. Here ye," his Liverpool accent boomed. "All those present for the trial of The State versus Aircraftsman Brown prey silene for the commencement of proceedings. Judge Archibald, Barnabas, Bartholomew, Bollocks presiding." I gave a cursory wave of my hand and nodded to the court.

The Clerk read out the charge and finished by addressing Brown directly.

"Do you plead guilty or not guilty?"

"Not Guilty." Brown replied.

The Prosecuting Counsel laid out its case and got several witnesses to testify. This was followed by the Defence Counsel presenting their case; they too, bringing forth one or two witnesses. With all arguments presented and tested, the Jury deliberated upon the facts as given. The fact that most of the witnesses were also members of the jury was conveniently overlooked. Within ten seconds they had reached their verdict.

Again the Clerk to the Court took the floor.

"Would the foreman of the Jury please stand." One of the group shuffled to his feet. "Does the Jury find the defendant guilty or not guilty?" the Clerk asked.

"Guilty," came the reply.

As solemnly as I could, I slowly placed a black pair of underpants upon my head, steepled my hands, leant slightly forward and looked directly at the defendant. Desperately, I fought to keep a straight face.

"Aircraftman Brown." I intoned. "You have been found guilty by twelve of your peers of the charge of lacking in personal hygiene. This is a horrendous and shocking crime which can only attract the most severe of punishments available to this court. You will be taken from here to a place of execution and hanged by the neck until dead. The sentence is to be carried out in five minutes time. God have mercy upon your soul."

Brown, still playing along, was escorted from the room and the rest of us went into action. We rearranged the furniture and created the so named place of execution. This consisted of Brown's bed mattress lying on the floor and below a formidable looking hangman's noose made out of a dozen or more black neck ties. These ties had been issued to us all as part of our uniform. I cannot remember what the noose was attached to at its ceiling end but it must have been a light fitting or something similar. Sitting on the mattress and directly below the noose, was an upturned metal bucket. This was the gallows. One of the lads played the part of the executioner by wearing a large paper bag over his head to replicate a hood. He had cut out two eye holes.

When we were ready, Brown was brought back into the room to the sound of one of our number tapping at an upturned can of floor polish with a spoon as if beating out a death march on a drum. Brown immediately saw the set up and his gaze turned towards the noose. He kept a tight face as he approached the mattress. Instructed to stand upon the bucket, he reluctantly did so. He still had not spoken a word. The executioner blindfolded him with a scarf or something similar and, as he did so, we swapped the noose for an almost identical one. The slight difference being that the second noose was connected to the ceiling by just one slender length of cotton.

The noose was placed around Brown's neck and tightened to a good fit. He could feel the tie material bight against his throat but had no idea that the noose had been swapped. As far as he was concerned, it was the one he had seen and which was very capable of choking someone to death. Brown continued with the play acting without comment. Looking back I wonder what he was thinking?

'This can't be real. They can't really hang me, but the noose looked solid enough.'

Someone recited The Lord's Prayer as the drum roll increased both in tempo and volume. With the prayer finished, the bucket was kicked out from beneath Brown's feet. He fell like a brick with a look of horror painted across his face. The noose tightened slightly and the cotton snapped. Brown fell onto the mattress and rolled off its edge onto the floor to a loud chorus of cheers and laughter. He lay on his back for a second or two in confusion before tearing off his blindfold. He loosened the noose and seeing the thread of cotton, realised what we had done.

"You Bastards," he said quietly. "You bloody bastards." He probably used a few other expletives as well. I will let you guess what they might have been.

I often wonder what happened to Brown as the last time I ever saw him was the day we all parted company to report to our individual technical training units. Fifty years on. I wonder if he still remembers the day he was 'hung by the neck'? The poor chap is probably still receiving counselling.

THE END

Did you know...

RAF Swinderby was located on the A46 Fosse Way, and situated between Newark in Nottinghamshire and Lincoln in Lincolnshire. The station started life in 1940 and was home to several bomber squadrons. Its offensive role though ended in 1964 when its role changed to RAF basic training for all male enlisted personnel. Female recruits arrived there in 1982 under an integrated training scheme. In 1993 though, the whole recruit training business, male and female, was shipped off to RAF Halton in Buckinghamshire. RAF Swinderby ceased to exist in 1995 when it was sold off. Today, where my accommodation block once stood, there is a green and pleasant field. The only remaining buildings are a few aircraft hangers which now form part of an industrial site. I believe that the airfield itself remains, but is inactive.

*****

It was only many years later when I was studying the 'ologies' at teacher training college that I realised how the RAF, as well as the other services, achieved the effect of team cohesiveness in just a few short weeks. They achieved this result by breaking the civilian down and remoulding and building him/her up again into a serviceman/woman.

If you are interested in sociology or organisational change, I recommend you look up Kurt Lewin's theory of the 'Change Process.' In this theory he describes change as a three-stage process… unfreezing, changing and refreezing. Quite an apt description really. The Service used this process by making us all completely dependent on it for every aspect of our lives. The Service determined when we woke up in the morning and what time we went to bed. It determined when we ate our meals. Where we spent each part of our day. What we learnt. When we could wear civilian clothes. When we had any free time and such.

I find the whole process quite fascinating really. In 1971 the RAF was helped in our reconditioning by the fact that the Post Office went on strike for seven weeks. This seven-week period covered the entire length of our six-week training. Post boxes were sealed and phone boxes locked up. As such, we could not communicate with our families or anyone else for that matter. Back then, mobile phones only existed in science fiction. The strike only served to add to our sense of isolation. It also helped, unwittingly, the RAF to break us down in preparation to build us back up again.

THE GREAT ESCAPE

I have no idea in what order you, the reader, is ploughing through my stories but you should, by now, realise that both my brother and myself were well used to having an air rifle in the house. My brother, older than myself by seven years, was given it as a Christmas present when he was a young teenager. He taught me how to load and shoot it and I was allowed to use it in the back garden. I was immediately hooked and hardly a day passed when I didn't practice my marksmanship.

We lived in a detached house with surrounding gardens. The back garden was quite a large one. Largely unseen from the main public road, its privacy made it ideal to double as a firing range and battle field where many a war was won and lost.

Nothing in the garden was safe. My mother's supply of wooden clothes pegs slowly dwindled as I shot them, one by one, from the clothes line. Her supply of potatoes and beetroot fared little better, especially the beetroot as they bled red juice when hit…just like blood! My father's bamboo bean sticks also took a pounding as I imagined them being the masts of enemy sailing galleons. His supply of electronic valves also suffered. These valves were very similar to narrow light bulbs and to my young mind, looked like spaceships. Great for intergalactic battles.

Most of my toys met their demise in that garden, smashed by an onslaught of lead pellets. Toy soldiers, toy cars, lorries, ships, planes and every plastic model kit that I had ever patiently assembled was eventually massacred. I even used to make crude looking military vehicles out of clay. I would collect a bucket of the stuff from the local fields and mould it by hand into tanks, trucks, field artillery and the like. I would then, with my mother's permission, bake them hard in her oven. When done, all that was left to do was lovingly paint them in a green and brown camouflage livery. These were great little targets as when hit, they exploded into dust.

When I was young, there was no such thing as colour television. In fact, I can remember a time when there was only one television station. The BBC. We were fed a diet of black and white programmes which included some classic war films which I still relish to this day even though some, sadly, have now been colourised. John Mills, Jack Hawkins, Noel Coward, Richard Attenborough et al were the heroes of the day. I always particularly liked the prisoner of war escape films which always had tense moments when the white circle of light from the searchlights slowly traversed the wooden huts; probing for trouble as the prisoners made their attempt to escape.

It was this type of film which was the genesis of a game that my brother and I invented. To the side of the house was a square shaped lawn which had a concrete path surrounding it. The edges of the lawn terminated in a low, castellated breeze block wall built two blocks high. This wall also doubled as the inner edge of the path; the outer edge being formed by the house itself, the garage and front boundary wall. This boundary wall separated the garden from the public road. Roadside it was about shoulder height but inside, because of a raised section of path, it was about waist height. It was this raised section of path which we used in our game.

The game was best played in the dark and involved one of us acting as the *escapee* and the other the *guard.* The guard was in control of the searchlight and the *machine gun.* The searchlight was a long, metallic hand torch which sported a powerful and narrow spot beam of light. This was taped to the underside of the air rifle's barrel so that if a target was spotted, a shot could quickly be dispatched.

Starting at the front garden gate, the escapee would attempt to crawl along the section of the path that ran along the length of the roadside boundary wall. The aim was to reach the far end of the path without being detected by the searchlight. The only thing that hid the escapee was the very low castellated breeze block wall. If any part of one's body or article of clothing showed, then the guard would quickly spot it as he slowly traversed the spot beam back and forth.

As far as the escapee was concerned, detection was announced by a pellet slamming into the high boundary wall above, showering him with small shards of stone and dust. At this point the game was over and my brother and I swapped places. We were not stupid and we always aimed high to avoid any injury, despite the temptation to go for the kill. To this day though, the inner face of that boundary wall must still bear the scars of that game. Pitted with pellet impact points and looking like the surface of the moon.

Another game we engaged in probably evolved from the one described above, though it required much more agility and a sense of timing. Our house looked out onto the playing fields of what was then, the village infants' school but which is now the village community centre. This consisted of a large area of grass with, at its far end, a row of very high, mature and thickly trunked trees. There were four or five of them and all had been planted in a neat row and spaced pretty much equidistant.

The game again involved an escapee and a guard though these terms, by now, had evolved into *target* and *shooter*. The shooter took position on the front lawn of the house which was about one hundred yards distant from the trees. As in the previous game, the shooter was in control of the searchlight and machine gun though this game was usually played during daylight hours.

The objective of the target was to get himself along the line of trees without being shot. This required agility, a short and fast burst of speed between trees and a sense of timing based upon how long it took the shooter to reload the rifle. The rule was that one fired low at the target's legs. This ensured no bodily damage as at the distance involved, a hit would be little more than a light impact. A short, sharp sting at worst. A hit though would be accompanied by a dramatic imitation of dying. Arms and legs would flail through the air, followed by a thespian fall to the ground, a series of rolls along the grass and an equally Oscar winning cry of death.

The success rate for the target reaching the far end tree was usually good, the anticipation of being hit more of a concern than actually being shot. During darkness the odds were even better as one could hop from tree to tree whilst the searching spot beam lingered elsewhere.

I wonder what would happen if such games were played in this day and age? Probably several SWAT teams would arrive, the village cordoned off and the searchlights of at least two police helicopters pinning the culprits down on the ground in a swathe of bright light. Where has all the fun gone eh?

THE END

Did you know...

An electronic valve, or vacuum tube, is an electronic 'switch' which was used to regulate current flow within an electrical circuit using a vacuum inside a sealed glass container. They looked very similar to electric light bulbs and were extensively used in television sets and early computers. They were the forerunners of the electronic transistor and the modern integrated circuits or "chips" as they are commonly known. As a television repair engineer, my father had hundreds of them lying around in his workshop but, as described above, many were blown apart by my brother and myself.

A CLEAN BREAK

If you have already read my story entitled "*The Fox Did It*," you might remember me mentioning that both sets of my grandparents had large back gardens which still exist to this day, albeit under new ownership. My paternal grandparents had the bigger of the two gardens consisting of vegetable patches, greenhouses, a small orchard and a large chicken run.

The bottom of the garden terminated in a narrow, winding river which separated the property from the agricultural land and the woods beyond. These fields and woods were an extension to the adventure playground and as long as one kept a wary eye out for the local farmer, my brother and I ventured about them fully at ease. We explored them with our bows and arrows, air rifles, home-made spears, catapults and the like.

We walked far and wide searching for bird nests amongst the hedgerows, collected hazel nuts in muslin bags, picked blackberries and also picked wild primroses, snow drops and bluebells when each was in season. These flowers were not protected as they are today. We picked these flowers for a reason. My grandmother used to sell small bunches of them along with cockles and home-made goodies at the local market. I can still remember as if it was yesterday, cutting the stems of these flowers to the correct length and then wrapping a small elastic band around them to form small bunches. These would be placed in the large wicker hand baskets that my grandmother used and then she would be off to the market for the day.

The local farmer whom I mentioned above shall remain nameless. He really was someone to avoid. To my young eyes he was ancient; a frightening figure who always seemed to carry a big stick with him. He had a great dislike of children trespassing upon his land. We both had several encounters with him when he would chase after us waving his stick and growling threats of "I know who you buggers are. I will be calling the police." Thinking back though, he was probably a nice old man who just liked to have fun chasing children off his land. I can't remember either of my grandparents saying a bad word about him. To me though, he was *very* frightening and to be avoided at all costs.

The other side of the river and directly opposite the bottom of the garden stood *"The Farm."* It wasn't a farm really, but just a collection of small buildings dominated by a large, open sided barn. The farmer himself lived in a house in the village, a house which we always hurried on by just in case he was about. We usually referred to this collection of buildings by the farmer's name but it was also referred to as *The Farm.*

The barn was a magnet for us boys. It had a large span of roof made from rust coloured corrugated tin sheets and which was supported on several cylindrical iron or steel pillars. It usually contained a healthy supply of bales of hay…cattle feed. These were rectangular in shape, quite heavy and bound tightly by strong string known as baler cord. The great thing to us boys was that these bales could be moved about like very large bricks to form castles, battlements, dens and the like. They also made excellent targets for when we were playing about with our bows and arrows. At the end of our fun though, we would always replace the bales in their original positions as we did not want to leave any clues behind as to our visitations!

My brother and I were staying at our grandparents' house when he suddenly appeared. "Follow me," he said. "I have something to show you." I followed him down through the garden and through the chicken run. We then crossed the river by hopping from one water lashed boulder to another to where the barn stood.

"Come on," he half whispered as he started to climb to the very top of the hay bales which was very near the top of the barn itself. He waited for me to catch up before he pulled away a bale exposing a rectangular tunnel into the mass of hay.

"Come and see what I have built," he said excitedly before disappearing into this mysterious tunnel. I followed and found myself inside a small secret den which my brother had constructed deep inside the pile of hay bales. Memory plays tricks I know, but I imagine that this 'cave' was about six foot square and about three foot high. I was greatly impressed with it and we put it to good use for some time afterwards when we wanted to 'disappear.' Neither my grandmother or the farmer ever found out about its existence.

I do remember though being very frightened when, whilst in the den, we heard a vehicle approach and stop amongst the buildings. My brother and I remained dead still and tight lipped as we listened to whoever was there, remove bales. I hoped and prayed that we would not be discovered and we both sighed with relief as the vehicle drove away. We had got away with it.

The experience was too close for comfort though and the decision was made to abandon our den, fill in the hole it had occupied and remove all evidence that it had ever existed. A point was reached in the den's demolition when we were left with a short wall of bales which needed to be re-stacked. We both lay on the top of this wall and using our own body weight, caused the wall to fall forward in a tumble, taking us both with it.

With whoops of delight we fell forward in a confusion of hay bales. I ended up on my back but when I eventually stopped moving, one of the heavy bales fell across my outstretched left arm. My cries of delight were soon replaced by a howl of pain. I cradled my arm with my good hand but that did nothing to relieve the searing pain. I was screaming in agony as tears filled my eyes and dripped off my cheeks. Ashen faced, my brother rushed over to me.

"Try to move your arm," he said urgently. I tried, but the limb was dead and useless.

Somehow, he managed to get me down to ground level and very slowly we retraced our steps back across the river, the chicken run and garden and back to the house.

We confronted our grandmother who, seeing the agony that I was in and confirming that the arm was dead and useless, decided to seek medical help. The next thing I can remember is being dragged by either my grandmother or my aunt along the lane that led from the house, down through the village to the bus-stop. My brother tagged along for a while, his face a picture of remorse. Whether or not I was taken to the doctor (Yes…one could see a doctor on the same day back then!) or straight to hospital I do not know. All I can remember with any clarity is staying in hospital on a children's ward for a full week with a heavy plaster cast attached to my arm. X-rays had determined that the bale of hay had fractured the bone of my upper arm (The Humerus) with a clean break.

I can't remember how old I was at the time, but I was certainly in single figures. At that age I was certainly an incredibly shy boy and would not willingly speak to anyone whom I did not know. I don't think I ever spoke to any of the other children on the ward and only responded to the nurses and doctors when they spoke to me. All I wanted was to go home to my mother. She visited me every evening and I spent the days anticipating her arrival and being left in tears when she left.

One odd thing I do remember with great clarity from my week in hospital is that, through the window opposite my bed, watching an electricity pylon being built in the far distance. Every day it crept higher and higher but I went home long before it was finished. I often wonder if that structure still exists.

I stayed home for a couple of weeks before I went back to school. Treatment of simple fractures were very different back then. These days one probably would not see a hospital bed. One would be strapped up and sent home with some painkillers and told to rest. Maybe just as well really!

THE END

Did you know…

The first use of *Plaster of Paris* as a means of immobilising an injured limb involved placing the affected limb in a wooden box and into which plaster of Paris was poured. Such a technique became favoured in Europe during the early 1800's. During the early 1900's, plaster of Paris bandages became available. These consisted of rolls of soft cloth which were impregnated with plaster of Paris powder which is a type of calcium phosphate, derived from gypsum. Water was then applied to the bandage which would then be wrapped around the injured limb. Within minutes, the bandage would begin to harden and 'set,' thus immobilizing the limb. Plaster of Paris is so named as the gypsum used to manufacture it was extensively mined near the city of Paris.

A MISS IS AS GOOD AS A MILE

I have always been totally useless at sports, especially at school. Even the best efforts of our sports teacher, Mr. Jones, made no difference. I could not play rugby. I could not play football. I could not play tennis or cricket, nor could I sprint, jump, swim or throw anything such as a javelin or discuss. I was equally inept in the gymnasium. I could not climb a rope or vault a horse, do press-ups or pull-ups and many a forged letter I wrote, supposedly from my mother, excusing me from sports on the grounds of some terrible disease or injury.

This total ineptness has always been due, in my opinion, to two things. A total lack of ability and a total lack of interest. Maybe if the interest was there then my meek and timid performances might have improved, but such interest did not exist and my school reports for the subject of Physical Education always had the comment... "Peter shows little interest and could do much better if he tried." I think Mr. Jones gave up on me in the end.

The one sport I did enjoy however, had nothing to do with school. This sport is known as Toxophily. "What?" I hear you ask. "Tox...what?". Please let me explain. Toxophily is the posh word for archery...bows and arrows and all that stuff. The word comes from the Greek language (Toxon = bow + Philos =loving). As such a Toxophilite is someone who loves bows or, in the usual sense, has an interest in Archery.

I was introduced to bows and arrows at an early age. Living in a rural part of Wales, my brother and I would fashion bows and arrows out of hazel sticks and use baler cord, nicked from hay bales which lay around in a local farmer's barn, for the strings. No ant hill of bale of hay was safe from attack. As a young teenager my brother acquired his first *real* bow. It was made from alloy metal and named "The Apollo". I only recently learned that the God of archery was, indeed Apollo, but whether or not this is why the bow was so named I have no idea.

My brother allowed me to use this bow and it is safe to say that using it steered me towards taking a keen interest in serious archery. Eventually I bought my own bow…a modern, wooden composite one. Of course, I made the cardinal mistake of buying a bow which was far too powerful for me. It seemed perfect in the shop where I bought it, but after taking it home and shooting off about a dozen arrows or more, my arms felt like falling off. Hence, I trapsed back to the same shop and purchased a second bow more suited to my meagre upper body strength.

I joined a local archery club where, after several attempts, I proudly managed to reach First Class Bowman status. Later in life I also qualified as an archery coach and with a generous grant from the local council, ran an archery club in the local community hall for several years. The club was a great success and attracted many youngsters from the village and beyond. Some of these youngsters went onto pursue the sport at university or elsewhere. None though, as far as I know, went onto win Olympic Gold!

One winter's weekend I was practicing my archery at a local beach. I had only just passed my driving test and with my new driving licence safely secure in my wallet, I borrowed my father's car and drove to the coast. It was a good place for target practice as the beach had a vast expanse of sand and was remote enough from roads not to attract a lot of people. Only the hardiest of walkers and swimmers and surfers would venture there, especially in the winter months. The beach was bordered by a large area of sand dunes behind which stood a camping and caravan park. These days the park is a very sophisticated one and contains many static caravans all lined up in neat rows like guardsmen.

Back in the day though, this park was in its infancy with little in terms of facilities. Back then it was used more by campers than by caravaners and in the summer months especially, the area would be dotted with tents of all shapes, sizes and colours. Several old fashioned 'rounded' caravans were dotted about here and there though, seemingly positioned wherever the owners fancied to put them.

On the day in question I had positioned a cardboard target near the top of one the sand dunes. I then walked back onto the beach and shot six arrows from a distance of about one hundred yards. Returning to the target, I was delighted to see it having been pierced by three of my arrows. A fourth stuck out of the sand nearby. The other two though I could not see at all. I searched and searched and eventually got down on my knees to claw aside the dense, spiky tufts of marram grass that commonly grew in the area.

After a lengthy search my two arrows remained lost. Disgruntled at losing two pieces of expensive equipment, I packed up my gear and headed back towards the car. I walked down the far side of the dune and eventually reached a ragged footpath which led to the car park. Off to my right stood a solitary caravan about thirty yards distant. It was in my peripheral vision and I took little notice. After all, it was just another caravan.

As I trudged along the path though, something colourful suddenly caught my eye. I turned my head and looked harder. The caravan was somewhat dilapidated and sad looking. Its once proud white sheen had long faded and the external walls and roof were freckled with small patches of black mould. This sorry state was just as well for there, protruding from the wall of the caravan, were my two arrows. Both had missed the target, skimmed through the grass at the top of the dune, sailed out over the space beyond and ended their flight with striking effect. One had pierced the caravan's door and the other was lodged just below the side window. It was the colourful 'fletchings' (feathers) at the top of each arrow that had caught my eye.

A hot flush of panic coursed through my very being and my initial instinct was to run. Instead, I looked around to see if anyone was about but only the light winds wandered around the dunes and rustled the grasses. No one had appeared from within the caravan and after a few moments of hesitation I stealthily approached, my heart pounding against my chest. The grimy curtains were fully drawn and no sound came from within.

Carefully and very slowly, I withdrew the arrow from the door. It came out easily. The second arrow though decided to put up a fight as it had stuck into something inside the caravan…the back of a bench seat I presumed. With much coaxing and twisting it eventually came free. I dropped both arrows amongst their companions in my shoulder quiver and took another quick look around for any witnesses. Again, only the wind stirred the airs. It was at this point that I did decide to run and run I did. I didn't stop until I reached the car. After hastily throwing my bow and arrows onto the back seat, I slammed the car into first gear, stamped on the accelerator and made a very fast exit.

THE END

Did you know…

Bows have been around for thousands of years and used for both hunting and war making. Archers on foot, or mounted on horses or chariots, were a major part of military forces until replaced by the invention of efficient firearms in the Late Middle Ages.

In the United Kingdom it took until shortly after the Norman invasion of 1066 when William, Duke of Normandy, had defeated the English King Harold at Hastings for the longbow to be developed into a weapon of war. A succession of Kings put great store in the bow as a military weapon and, to ensure that there was a steady supply of skilled archers, passed laws to ensure that men of a certain age regularly practiced their skills.

Newly invented games thought to be frivolous were banned as it was thought by the 'powers to be' that men, rather than wasting time playing them, should be practicing archery instead. Such "frivolous" games included football, bowls, golf, tennis and cockfighting. Over the years such laws have been repealed by successive Acts of Parliament. The last remnants were repealed by the Betting and Gaming Act 1960.

I suppose that in these current modern-day times of Trident submarines, nuclear missiles and star wars, it is easy to dismiss the bow and arrow as a primitive weapon. Back in the middle ages though the bow was the Trident missile of its day.

*****

Composite bows are made from different layers of wood and horn which are laminated together with glue under great pressure. Such bows are stronger, more flexible and are able to store more energy than a bow made from a single piece of wood.

*****

The amount of force required to pull back a bow is called its 'weight' and is measured in pounds force (pbf). My second bow had a weight of 40pbf whereas the archers of the Middle Ages drew bows of around 75pbf with ease...They must have been powerful men.

MUD, MUD, GLORIOUS MUD

If you have already read my story entitled '*Second Place*', you might remember me describing myself as non-athletic. I hated 'gym' at school and presented many a forged letter, supposedly signed by my mother, to the Physical Education (P.E.) teacher excusing me from what I considered to be dangerous and sweat laden activities. My reluctance to engage in P.E. was due to a complete lack of interest combined with a total lack of talent. I was useless at Rugby, Cricket, Soccer and all other games. Despite being well over six foot two inches tall I couldn't sprint, jump, skip, throw a javelin or discus and deservedly was always one of the last to be picked to join a particular team.

In the gymnasium my performance was even worse. I could not vault a horse; do press ups of chin ups and no way could I climb a rope. The one thing I could do though was run long races (Again, I refer you to my story '*Second Place*'). I could plod along for hours enjoying the relative solitude, my fantasies and my thoughts.

Away from the rigours of school sports though, my passion from very early in my teens was long distance walking. As the years began to mature me this passion became more and more embedded and became a serious past time. I don't know why I developed this interest. I suspect that it was a gradual evolution, having started by the fact that I was born and brought up in the rural area of Gower in South Wales. Some of my earliest memories are of tramping across the local fields and exploring the woods whilst trailing along behind my older brother.

I soon reached an age when I was able to start exploring on my own. At first my solitary excursions into the countryside were fairly local affairs but as my confidence grew, my wanderings stretched further afield and became longer. I purchased Ordinance Survey maps of Gower and set out to walk every public footpath marked on the maps covering the peninsula. I would study the maps and work out circular routes either starting and ending at home or, once I had learnt to drive, from car back to car wherever it was parked.

After completing all those mapped paths as well as other, unofficial ones, I had the idea of trying to walk the entire perimeter of the peninsula (As far as I can work out from the maps, fifty or so miles) along its coastal paths within twenty-four hours. This took a bit of planning and I mentally worked out that it could be done considering the mileage and the twenty-four-hour time window...an average walking speed of about two to three miles/hour would be needed. 'Could I do it?' I asked myself.

On the summer's day in question, a Saturday, I left home at exactly 5:00 am. when it was just light enough to walk safely. With a small back pack containing sandwiches, chocolate, a flask of hot tea, a whistle and a torch, I set off. Progress was good, but at about half way I began to really feel the pain in the thigh muscles. I kept my head down and kept going. The only way I managed to put one booted foot in front of the other was the thought that each step was taking me closer to the finishing line. 'Besides,' I thought, 'If I stopped, my legs would seize up and I would never get going again.' I completed the trip in just under twenty-two hours and staggered into a boiling hot bath in the early hours of Sunday morning. I had done it!

It took a few days before I could walk properly again, but I wore the smile that goes along with a sense of achievement. That walk still fills me with pride and has always been one of my claims to fame. I often wonder if that feat has ever been duplicated by anyone else? Most of the route I walked is now part of the all-Wales coastal path (870 miles) but I still like to think that I remain the only person to have completed it within twenty-four hours. Maybe no-one else would be so crazy as to contemplate such a task?

Then I discovered national trails. These, as the name suggests, are very long walks which usually take a week or more to complete. Apparently, at the time of writing, there are sixteen such trails in the UK. Over the years I polished off elven of them, including the 'big one'…The Pennine Way (268 miles.) I did each of all eleven walks in 'one hit' so to speak. All, that is, with the exception of The Penine Way which, due to the time available and the distance involved, I completed in two hits.

I was a purist in all these walks. No youth hostels or bed and breakfasts for me. I carried a back pack weighing some thirty-five pounds containing a tent, sleeping bag, a gas stove, a billie can and other bits of pieces. It was a case of head down and go for it! Daily distances were governed by the position of camp sites where there were proper facilities and a nearby pub where one could get a decent meal. Fifteen to twenty miles a day would have been the norm though.

With all of my walks which spanned many years, I never really got into any difficulties or dangerous situations. Fatigue and aching shoulders and limbs were the norm, but actual danger I never experienced…. except once!

I was coming towards the end of a long days' walk on Gower and decided to take a short cut across a large, open common. Reaching the common's far side I entered a wood of old oak trees. The wood was unfamiliar to me but I decided to forge on through it. All was well until a very wet bog barred my way. There was no way around it without a lengthy detour so I decided to plan a way across. I had encountered many bogs in my time and, with the help of my trusty walking stick, I had always managed to cross them without too much difficulty… a boot full of water at worst.

I tested the bog with my walking stick, searching out the most solid tufts of grass that grew out of it. These tufts I intended to use as stepping stones. Using my stick to help my balance, I carefully set forth. I soon realised that I had bitten off more than I could chew but it was impossible to turn back. I struggled forward and, without warning, I fell through the bog up to my waist. Terror gripped hold of me like a vice and in my panic, I started thrashing about. The more I struggled though, the further I sank and I had visions of slowly sinking and drowning…my worst nightmare.

Controlling my fear, I stopped moving whilst trying to clear my head. Taking in my surroundings I looked around for an escape route. I noticed that a long, gnarled branch from one of the oaks stretched out over the bog and was about two foot above my head. I was just able to reach up and touch it but it was too thick to grip onto. Then I had an idea!

Pulling my walking stick out of the quagmire I managed to position it over the branch and grab it with both hands. Then, as if doing pull ups on a bar in a gymnasium, I heaved and heaved. Luckily my stick was thick and sturdy and able to take the force. Inch by slow inch I pulled myself up and freed both of my legs from the sucking mud. My problems were far from over though for there was no solid ground to stand on and my strength was ebbing fast.

I had read somewhere that if one was caught in quicksand then one should fall lengthwise onto the surface and quickly roll oneself out onto firm ground. This I did…splash! Taking my stick with me I started rolling as soon as I entered the watery slime. Over and over I went, my face sometimes completely submerged. I reached the solid far bank with my heart trying to thump its way out of my chest. With most of my body still submerged I clung onto two tufts of grass, completely exhausted. There I lay, waiting for my heart rate and breathing to return to normal and the fear and panic to subside.

Like a wounded crab, I crawled out onto dry land, rolled over onto my back and gazed up through the branches to the clear sky beyond. I have no idea how long I stayed there but it seemed to be for ages. The time came to take stock of myself. I was soaked to the skin and black with mud. By scooping water out of the bog with my hand, I washed off as much slime as possible. I then trudged off home a little wiser and with visions of a hot, luxurious bath dancing around in my thoughts. I received a few odd looks and a few comments as I entered the village but 'what the hell' I thought. At least I had lived to tell the tale.

THE END

Did you know...
The Wales Coast Path is a long-distance walking trail which follows, or runs close to, the coastline of Wales. It was officially opened in 2012 and runs for 870 miles from the River Dee in North Wales to Chepstow in the south. It boasts being the first coast path in the world to cover the entire length of a country's coastline.

*****

I have always had a phobia about mud. As a young child I would not go near the stuff. I remember that whenever my mother took me with her cockle picking out on the local mud flats, she had to take a cardboard box with her for me to stand in whilst she set to work. The reason for the box was that if I had seen my toes sink into the mud, I would have gone ballistic with fear.

WHITE OUT

If you have already read my story entitled '*Mud, Mud, Glorious Mud,*' then you will know that a lifetime passion of mine *was* long distance walking. I emphasise 'was' because in 1992, at the age of forty-three, I was diagnosed as having chronic heart failure. That brought an end to my walking adventures. These days I cannot even walk up a flight of stairs without getting breathless and with my heart thumping in protest.

Back in the day though I was a prodigious walker, both locally and further afield and I trekked several of the UK's national trails. I also did a lot of interesting walking when I lived and worked in Australia. There, my boots trudged along open bush land, through dense rain forests, over snow-capped mountain ranges and kicked up dry dust as I hiked the bone-dry deserts. I also left footprints in the snows of Antarctica when I briefly worked there as a research assistant.

One particularly exciting walk was when, as part of a group, I walked the infamous Kokoda trail in Papa New Guinea. This 60-mile-long trail is well known to students of the Pacific war in World War Two, for it was the location of several battles in 1942 between the Japanese and mainly Australian forces.

My walks back in the UK covered all kinds of terrain. Undulating countryside, rugged coastline, open moorland, green canopied forests and woods, tide lapped estuaries and marshes as well as the high mountain regions. Over the years I climbed the famous 'three peaks. Snowdon (3,560 feet), Scafell Pike (3,210 feet) and Ben Nevis (4,413 feet). If you don't already know, these mountains are the highest in Wales, England and Scotland respectively, with the summit of Ben Nevis being the highest point in the UK. In fact, I have summited Ben Nevis twice. Both times were in September and both times the last mile or so had me trudging through thick snow and fighting against stinging blizzards. I often wonder if the summit is ever free of snow?

Snowdon, I have summited many times. There are six classic routes up the mountain, each of which I have walked several times. My usual strategy was to walk up one route and descend by another. I also did several alternative routes, including the famous Crib Goch (Red Ridge) route.

This route is akin to walking along the edge of a razor blade. At points the bouldered path is little more than two feet wide with almost vertical drops either side of several hundred feet. There have been many fatalities there over the years. The advantage of this route is that one reaches altitude very quickly. At its high point it is 3,028 feet above sea level and just short of Snowdon's summit of 3,560 feet.

The one and only time I walked it, I left the car at about 5:00 am and managed to reach Crib Goch's summit in time to witness the sun make its grand appearance into the world. At that time of day I was completely alone and I stood, transfixed in awe, as the growing orb of sunlight painted the surrounding mountains in hues of gold and yellow. At the narrowest part I lost my nerve and crawled along for about one hundred feet on my hands and knees. One gust of strong wind, I thought, would make this my last walk. Sometimes, cowardice is the best option.

This story 'Whiteout' concerns one of my ascents to the summit via what is known as The Pyg track. I had used this path a few times before and, as such, I knew it to be the most rugged of the six classic routes. Near its summit end it joins with The Miner's Track which traverses a parallel route but which is on the valley floor below. From where the two paths meet, there is a short, sharp climb up to the ridge which then leads to Snowdon's summit. The last part of this climb to the ridge is via steps which have been cut into the solid rock.

I have summited Snowdon thirteen times in my life but only on three occasions have I ever had a view from the summit. Usually, the summit was shrouded in cloud and the day relating to this story was no exception. As I started climbing the steps, I began to enter the clinging, white mist. I stepped onto the ridge. Pausing for breath, I felt good that the hard work had been done. From this point on, it was just a relatively short and easy walk to the summit.

Standing there I was completely enveloped in thick, white cloud. Complete whiteout. I could not even see the ground beneath my feet. Suddenly I became completely disorientated. The hot blush of fear gripped me as I realised that I was only feet, perhaps only inches from the precipice that I had just climbed up. 'But in what direction was that precipice? Was it behind me? In front? To my left? To my right?' I had no idea.

I forced myself to calm down and started to prod the invisible ground around me with my trusty walking stick. It was solid and firm but in what direction do I now walk? I have always been fascinated by maps and ever since I was a young teenager, I have been proficient in map and compass work. On walks such as this, I always carried both map and compass, just in case. I knew that I needed to walk West to safety and my new, quicky thought up plan, was to follow this heading until I met the mountain railway which ran from the village of Llanberis to the summit.

I waited a few seconds for my compass needle to settle on North before very slowly walking West. Before each step I prodded the ground in front of me, just to make sure it was there. In this fashion I slowly prodded and stumbled my way across the mountain. The damp, white mist was unrelenting and progress was slow. My sense of panic completely evaporated though as my stick made contact with something hard and solid. It was one of the rails of the railway track which suddenly took form in front of me. I was safe and I knew, at last, where I was. I gave a sigh of relief and congratulated myself for a job well done.

From there I just followed the railway track to the summit whilst keeping one ear cocked for approaching trains. As I trudged forever upwards through the cloud I felt very alone. As if I was the only person on the planet. In fact, I had not spotted another human being all day. Imagine my surprise upon reaching the summit railway terminus to see ghostly figures moving about in the swirling white mists. People! Masses of people. The place was packed with climbers, walkers and those who had either climbed via other routes or had journeyed up by train.

I had imagined myself to be the only walker there and seeing such a crowd of humanity left me feeling somewhat deflated. Fortunately there was an empty table in the summit café where I rested my aching limbs and calmed right back down to normality after my very recent dance with danger. Which route I took down the mountain that day I do not remember. I made it back down safely in one piece though and able to tell this tale of my adventure in the cloud.

THE END

Did you know…
The Kokoda trail is in Papa New Guinea and is 60 miles long. It traverses through rugged and isolated mountain and jungle terrain, connecting Buna on the north coast to Port Moresby in the south. The Japanese army used the trail in an attempt to seize Port Moresby, thereby isolating Australia from the United States (Back then, Papa New Guinea was then the Australian Territory of Papua). The Japanese almost reached their objective but finally withdrew when they outran their supply chain and as a consequence of losses suffered elsewhere in the Pacific War.

*****

In Welsh folklore the summit of Snowdon marks the tomb of Rhitta Gawr, a giant who ruled over the area. Legend tells that he wore a cloak made of the beards of warriors whom he had slain. He was eventually killed by King Arthur after wanting to add Arthur's beard to his collection. He was buried on top of the mountain. This story is claimed to be the reason that the Welsh name for Snowdon is Yr Wyddfa, which literally means 'the tumulus' (a mound of earth or stones raised over a grave).

*****

The Pyg track is a strange name I know, but my research has uncovered several possible origins. Some claim that the path is named after 'Pen Y Hostel' (The Hostel Head) by climbers who stayed there and from where the track starts. I can't see the connection myself though. Others say that the track is named after Bwlch Y Moch (The pass of pigs) since the path crossed it. Others claim the path was used to carry 'Pyg' (Black Tar) to the mountain's copper mines. Who knows eh?

GOING WITH THE FLOW

Those of you readers who might have already cast your eyes over my story entitled '*A Load of Hot Air*' will already know that I spent a large chunk of my life living and working in Australia as a teacher. Teaching in Australia was all very informal. Teachers were known to pupils by their first names. Everyone dressed casually and on particularly hot days, it was perfectly acceptable to abandon a lesson and spent the time outside playing sports. This social atmosphere also existed in the staff room. Teachers, administrative staff and the school hierarchy were as one big family. We were all 'mates', the epitome of Australian culture. It was this familial culture that led to the events which relate to this story.

I was sitting in the staff room when I was approached by Loui, one of the young science teachers.

"Hi Mate," Loui said as he sat beside me. "Do you fancy going white water rafting with John and myself down in 'The Snowies'? John has a raft that can do the job and we'd take the girls (wives) with us if they are up for it."

"Sure," I replied. "I'm definitely interested, but I'd have to check it out with Maria (my wife) first." As such, the die was cast and a few weeks later at the start of the summer school holidays (December), Loui, John, myself with all three wives, Rebecca, Heather and Maria, headed south in two cars with John towing the trailer containing the bright yellow inflatable raft. Incidentally, forty years on as I write this story, I cannot remember the real names of the other two wives, but Rebecca and Heather read and sound just fine to me.

'The Snowies' relate to 'The Snowy Mountains' which are situated in southern New South Wales (NSW). Throughout the year the mountains and their surrounding area form a vast area of wilderness which attracts skiers, campers, walkers, fishermen, canoeists and white-water rafters such as our small group. There are several resorts that service this area and we were headed for the township of Thredbo where the main resort is situated.

Our adventure was to take place on the Thredbo river. Located in the Perisher Valley (a name we should have taken note of as things turned out), the river is approximately twenty-five miles long. We only planned to raft a short section of it, a section which Loui, who had arranged the whole trip, assured us was completely safe to navigate!

We had booked three chalets there for a two-night stay. Day one would consist of travelling there. Day two would be for the expedition itself and day three for the return trip home. The chalets were typical, single story alpine type log cabins, very luxurious and very comfortable and the food served in the restaurant was heavenly. On the morning of day two we all awoke bright eyed and bushy tailed, ready for the big adventure ahead. The plan was that only five of us would travel the river. Heather, John's wife, elected to stay behind in order to pick us all up at the end of our journey and bring us back to Thredbo.

The river looked spectacular in the early morning sunshine, the light bouncing off the placid water in soft diamond like bursts. We launched the raft and with a cheery wave to Heather, we gently pushed ourselves away from the bank. The river at this point was very shallow and I remember walking on the stony river bed as I pushed the dinghy out into deeper water before clambering aboard.

Loui and John gently paddled us out into mid-stream where the weak current took hold of us with its soft caress. Our journey began as the flow of water pushed us down river. The river was gentle, the placid waters and the brilliant sunshine filling us all with both delight and confidence. We were loving it and we all looked forward to a pleasant day ahead.

The river remained calm and placid for quite a while as it took us gently downstream. The paddles in the dinghy were only needed to steer us around the odd boulder or two that protruded above the surface. They were not needed to provide propulsion. Occasionally we would get stuck behind a large boulder, and when this happened, one or two of us would jump into the shallow water and push the dinghy free of the obstruction before quickly clambering back in.

As we travelled forever forward, we delighted in watching wild kangaroos bounce about on either bank. Some just stood standing on their haunches and watched us glide past with a threatening look. Even the odd emu appeared but they seemed not to even notice us. Instead, they awkwardly strutted about looking for grubs and such to eat. At one point a sea eagle appeared above us, easily riding the updrafts of the ever-warming morning air. It circled and wheeled but always kept its gaze on the strange creatures below. It eventually decided it did not want us for a mid-morning snack and quietly glided away without even one flap of its powerful wings.

Without us realising it, the river began to pick up pace. Soon, us lads were feverishly using the paddles to avoid boulders. The flow of water was now getting powerful and time and time it wedged us up against the larger obstructions. These stoppages were beginning to get irksome and costing us in time. The day plodded on into the afternoon and the pace of water ever quickened. At narrower points in the river the water flowed faster and we screamed with delight as we shot through, bouncing around at the river's want.

We piled up against a very large boulder which sat right in the middle of the river and we became stuck fast. Thank goodness we had come to a sudden stop for just beyond the boulder, the water dropped suddenly away in a steep and long drop to a lower level about a hundred feet below us. Not a waterfall really, but pretty close. It was decided that the drop was far too risky and that the boat should be allowed to go over this drop on its own with us all climbing down on foot.

The immediate problem though was that we were being held solidly against the boulder by the force of the water and that we were a good distance from either bank. We all climbed onto the boulder and us three lads heaved and pushed at the boat for what seemed ages. Suddenly it broke free from its prison and shot over the edge of the watery precipice. We watched it go in awe, all of us probably thinking 'I could have been in that'. To our relief the dinghy reappeared far below in one piece. It bobbed about in a placid pool and seemed to be calling to us 'Come on then, I'm waiting.'

We still had the problem though that all five of us were stranded in the middle of a fast-flowing river. We had kept both paddles with us and by using these as walking sticks, we all, after much passing and throwing, made it safely to shore but not without some difficulty. Reaching the shore myself I looked up at the sky. Daylight was just passed its best and I suggested to all that we had better hurry if we were going to meet up with Heather before it got dark. In Australian latitudes it gets dark very quickly. There is no dusk as such and it can take only half an hour or so to go from bright daylight to complete and utter darkness. I didn't voice my concern, but I didn't think that we would get much further before darkness stopped us in our tracks.

Retrieving the dinghy we set off again. The river remained wild and rapid with progress remaining slow, once again, because of boulders. Again we got stuck. Louis and John jumped overboard and pushed and heaved until the dinghy broke free. The water was very fast and neither had time to climb back aboard. I can picture them now, growing further away and smaller as both girls and myself sped away.

The river soon narrowed and the water increased violently in speed. The classic venturi effect. We held on tight as we surged forward in the flow. To our left there was a high, vertical cliff and to the right, massive boulders. The rocks were worn smooth by the passage of time and the erosion of relentless water. The dinghy surged through the narrow gap and slid up a curved rock wall as the river turned ninety degrees. The speed and the angle forced the dinghy up on its side at which point I fell out.

The dinghy disappeared at great speed as I floundered in a quiet but very deep pool. With the crash of the fast-flowing white water singing in my ears, I swam to the far side of the pool and climbed out. Scrambling to the top of the glassy surfaced boulder, I desperately sought out the dinghy and the girls. To my great relief I saw them straight away. The dinghy was bobbing about in a very large and quiet pool into which the raging torrent we had just negotiated emptied into.

Both girls were swimming safely towards a small, pebbly beach. I shouted back to Loui and John that we were all ok and then surveyed the immediate surroundings as the girls reached the shore. The pool was fronted by a wall of ancient shiny rock which held back the water like a dam. In the middle of this natural barricade there was a very narrow cleft through which the river went on its way with a roar. We later learnt that once through the cleft, the water fell vertically into a white mist far below. Thank God for the wall and the pool. No one would have survived if they had gone over.

Loui and John caught up and we all sat on the pebbles and discussed our situation. It was at this point that I realised that I had lost one of my shoes. The day now felt dank and forbidding, a feeling not buoyed by the single threatening note of the waterfall nearby. The dinghy and paddles were still floating about but there was no way we could continue our boating journey. We had started out on a river that was smooth, calm and inviting. Here the river was angry. Angry that we mere humans had dared to challenge it. It was getting the better of us.

The light by now was fading fast and we knew that we only had thirty minutes maximum before it became completely dark. This was a time when mobile phones were not very common, though thinking back, I doubt if we would have got a phone signal considering where we were.

There was only one thing to do and that was to try and walk out. We decided to stay as one group for safety and with me wearing two socks borrowed from the lads on my shoeless foot, we set off down river. We left the dinghy where it was and I have often since wondered what happened to it. It might still be bobbing around in that pool for all I know.

There was no footpath as such. Just a vague kind of animal trail that crashed through the bush. We trudged on and on and suddenly stumbled on a dirt track that led to the river bank from high above us. Our hearts lightened somewhat as the track, over grown and disused as it was, meant civilization might be close by. We followed the track up the steep incline, the light fading with each passing second.

Eventually the track forked in two and we decided to turn right. This track soon petered out and became lost in thick bush so we backtracked. The second fork was much better and it became easier to walk the further on we went. We eventually reached a fairly large clearing which was dominated by a massive old gum tree. It was now almost pitch black so we decided that we would spend the night there rather than risk walking along a track we couldn't see and didn't know.

We were wet, cold and hungry but just had to get on with it. We lay down on the bare earth in a heap of bodies with the girls on the inside so that they could best benefit from the combined body heat. I can honestly say that it was the coldest night I have ever had in my life. I lay in the foetal position with my hands tucked deep into my arm pits. All I was wearing was a thin wet suit and one battered shoe, all of which were very wet. My teeth chattered all night and if I did sleep at all, it was probably fitfully.

We lay there wondering what Heather was doing. She was probably back in her warm and cosy bed at Thredbo worrying herself sick after we had not turned up as expected. Had she called the police? Were there search teams out looking for us right now? There was no way to answer either question.

At the first hint of daylight we all got up and started jumping on the spot and swinging our arms in an attempt to get warm and restart our circulation. When ready, we continued along the track not knowing where it would take us. It was an easy walk with forests of gum trees either side and outcrops of sand stone dotted here and there. The further along we walked, the track showed more and more evidence that it was at least used. Hopefully civilisation and salvation would be around the next corner.

Turning the next corner there was no salvation waiting the other side. There was though, perched on the top of an outcrop of rock … wait for it… a dentist's chair! We thought we had gone mad. Here we were, lost in a wilderness forest and there, facing us was a lone dentist chair. Absolutely crazy!

Recovering from this bizarre sight, we plodded on. We must have walked another hour before one of the girls shouted. "Look." She pointed straight ahead. "A house. A bloody beautiful house." Our gazes followed her finger and, sure enough, dead ahead a lone house started to emerge from the gum trees that surrounded it. We had endured. We had suffered. We had conquered. Salvation was, at long last, at hand.

It was a very sorry and bedraggled bunch that arrived at the door. We knocked but there was no answer. We knocked several times but to no avail. There was no vehicle about which, considering the remoteness of the place, confirmed that no one was at home. We hummed and hared trying to decide what to do. Considering the pitiful state that we were in, it did not take us long to decide to break in. Loui punched his elbow through a window pane and reached in to undo the latch. He then climbed in and eventually opened the door.

We all piled in and sat down in various states of distress and fatigue. There was no phone to call anyone, but there was plenty of food and the open fire had been laid. Soon the fire was blazing and a hot meal provided. After repleting himself, John decided to continue on to find a phone to contact Heather. The rest of us chilled out whilst keeping a wary look out for the house's owner.

A few hours later our hearts leapt in alarm as we heard a vehicle approach. Thankfully it was not the owner. It was Heather with John sitting beside her. I think we all gave a sigh of relief in perfect unison. We left a note for the owner explaining everything and which contained Loui's contact details. We all then piled into John's vehicle and headed back to Thredbo for a well-deserved shower and a long kip. Heather had contacted the police but they had suggested everyone wait a while as they felt sure that we would turn up. She immediately informed them that we had.

Returning home we forgot all about it and soon the whole incident faded into the realms of a bad dream. About a month later the bill arrived. The owner of the house, quite rightly, wanted full compensation for the window we had broken and for the food we had consumed. Loui, John and I chipped in to make up the full amount. The house, by the way, was the holiday home of a city dentist. At least that explained the chair sitting out on the rocky outcrop. We had not gone mad after all.

THE END

Did you know…
'The Snowies' relate to 'The Snowy Mountains' which are situated in southern New South Wales (NSW). They are the tallest range of mountains in mainland Australia and form part of the continent's Great Dividing Range. They contain Australia's five tallest peaks all of which are above 6,890 feet with Mount Kosciusko being the tallest at 7,310 feet. On another occasion I climbed Mount Kosciusko. It is not a challenging mountain to climb and its summit can be easily reached via reasonably well-defined footpaths. Its main attraction is that it is the highest point of mainland Australia and I remember boasting to my Australian colleagues on the walk that back home, in Wales, Mount Kosciusko would be

called a 'hill'. At that point I think I became known as a 'whinging pom'.

The 'Snowies' have large natural snowfalls every winter (June through to September) and is one of the main centres of the Australian skiing industry, containing all four snow resorts in NSW. Our rafting trip took us south to the town of Thredbo which is the main resort in the area. Thredbo started life in the 1860's as a gold mining town. Tourism arrived in the early 1900's as a result of the excellent snow falls and opportunities for skiing. In the summer if offers trails for walkers and bikers and excellent fishing and water sports in the Thredbo river.

IT'S WHO YOU KNOW THAT MATTERS

Have you ever experienced a moment when, in your mind's eye, you see your entire career crumble to pieces due to some disaster of your own making? Well I have! It didn't happen to me in my teens. It happened when I was in my late twenties. I was in the Royal Air Force and, at the time of 'my moment', I held the rank of Sergeant. My trade designation was that of Aircraft Fitter Weapons which, to put it simply, meant that my job entailed working with things that went bang! It was a very interesting trade to be in as, depending upon which RAF station I was at, I might be working on anything from hand guns right up to nuclear bombs and everything else in between. Big toys for big boys.

I had just been promoted to the rank of Sergeant and posted to a base which will remain nameless. Let's just call it 'An airfield somewhere in England', just like those old-World War Two black and white movies sometimes do. With my brand new three stripes on my uniform weighing my arms down with their importance, I arrived at my new station and reported to the guard room. I was allocated a room in the Sergeants' Mess and quickly settled in before reporting for duty at the armament section on the base. A 'Section', by the way is RAF jargon for 'department'. I had been advised by my boss at the station I had just left to walk into my new role as if I had been a Sergeant for years. Young airmen, he told me, can smell fear. It was good advice which I always passed onto new sergeants in turn.

Moving into the Sergeants' Mess was a big step in one's career. It was just like joining a new brotherhood. One was now a non-commissioned officer (NCO). A senior manager with all that that entailed. For the first time in one's career one was living with, eating with and socialising with other

NCO's. Other Sergeants, Chief Technicians, Flight Sergeants and, the mightiest of all, Warrant Officers.

These NCOs ran the day-to-day business of various sections around the base, technical and non-technical. Up until one reached the rank of Sergeant, if one wanted anything done, especially something of a personal nature, then one had to follow the correct procedure or protocol. Once in the Mess though, one just had a quiet word with the appropriate person. As such, much business could be conducted over lunch or dinner, in the lounge over coffee or over a game of snooker. In fact, I have always likened the Sergeants' Mess to that of the corporate golf course in terms of business deals. It took a while to find out which person ran what section but, over time, I managed to befriend some useful people.

On the day relevant to this story, I was responsible for running what was called 'the twilight' shift. This shift started at 1700 hrs (5:00pm) when the day shift finished, and ended at the conclusion of the day's flying programme when the last aircraft had landed. This was a good shift to be on as usually we were finished by 2200 (10pm) and often somewhat earlier. The twilight shift operated with a minimum of personnel as most of the day's flying had been completed by the time this shift started. Our role, if needed by any of the squadrons, was to remove and/or fit bombs or infra-red dischargers as needed.

It was winter and, as it turned out, was thankfully very dark. I had been tasked to remove two infra-red dischargers from a late home Vulcan bomber and to safely 'put them to bed'. Myself and a junior engineer named Jamie went out to do the job in one of our section's land rovers and towing a trolley behind us. These trolleys were very long and heavy pieces of equipment and specifically designed to receive the infra-red dischargers once removed from the aircraft.

Between us we successfully removed both the dischargers and checked that they were positioned safe and snug on the trolley. We then set off back to our section with our blue light flashing and with myself relaxing in the land rover's passenger seat. We were way out in the middle of the airfield in pitch darkness when there was one very loud bang as the land rover lurched forward violently.

"What the hell was that?" I shouted to no one in particular. My question was quickly answered by yet another heavy bang and a second violent push forward. As Jamie braked hard, we both watched in horror as the trolley, with both dischargers sitting on top, slowly overtook us.

"We've got one of those," I said in shock, but the humour of my remark quickly evaporated as the trolley began to fade from our headlights and disappear into the night. We were on a downward camber in the road and the trolley happily continued along it in the general direction of another parked Vulcan aircraft. It wasn't moving very fast but the sheer weight of it all meant that anything it might hit would probably come off worst.

Fortunately, the trolley ran off the metalled roadway onto the damp grass and came to a stop. Catching up with it we both quickly exited the land rover and checked both dischargers and the trolley for damage. Fortunately there was none. Our investigation revealed that the steel pin securing the trolley to the land rover had not been fitted properly and had dislodged itself. This had caused the trolley to break free and smash into the land rover. Jamie had fitted the pin but, as senior person, it was my responsibility to have checked that all was well.

Even though the dischargers and trolley had escaped unscathed, the land rover told a different story. Its back door was badly caved in and its rear bodywork had several serious dents. The image that has stuck in my mind all these years though is that of the vehicle's right-hand cluster of rear lights. They had been smashed to bits, buckled and hanging free on an electrical cable.

Eventually we reached our section and placed the trolley in its proper place for the following day shift to deal with as was usual. On the very slow journey back from the scene of the crime though, my mind was racing as how to minimise the damage to both of our careers. This incident would surely result in a 'Technical Charge', a black mark which would stay on one's service record for ever. I am not a particularly religious man, but I thanked God that the incident had happened in the darkness of that winter's evening. If it had happened during daylight and probably witnessed by many, Jamie and myself would have been shot, hanged, drawn and quartered.

I then had an idea. I drove the land rover to the Motor Transport section just to see if they could help out at all. Now, this is where living in the Sergeants' Mess *really* paid off. Running the Section that evening was a Chief Technician whom I knew well as we often played snooker together. He looked at the damage, shook his head in disbelief and told me to leave the vehicle with him.

By 0900 hrs (9:00am) that land rover had a new back door, the dents had been knocked out of the bodywork and a new light cluster fitted. I could have fainted with relief. I had got away with it. Both Jamie and myself would live to fight another day. I owed that Chief Technician loads and he never let me forget it either!

As the morning wore on though my conscience got the better of me. Even though I was not due on shift until evening, I gritted my teeth and went to see my boss, Warrant Officer Dave Angell, just before lunch time. I got on well with Dave. He, too, lived in the Mess and he also enjoyed a game of snooker. I stood in front of his desk and confessed all. Leaning back in his chair he listened patiently and without interruption, his fingers and thumbs steepled on his chest. When I had run out of words there was a pregnant pause as Dave weighed up the situation in his own mind. He turned his head and stared out of the window for a moment letting me wonder and suffer. Then he looked me straight in the eye. His face creased into a hint of a smile as he nodded towards the door of his office.

"Peter," he said with a question hanging off the word. "Fuck Off, will you?" All was well with the world again.

THE END

Did you know…

This new posting of mine was to a bomber station. The station operated Vulcan bombers. The Vulcan was a jet powered delta wing high altitude bomber which formed part of the RAF's 'V Force' along with the Victor and Valiant bombers. These three aircraft formed the UK's airborne nuclear deterrent during much of the Cold War. The Vulcan entered service with the RAF in 1956 and continued in service until it was retired in 1984.

*****

An 'infra-red discharger' was a large, oblong metal box which contained several dozen infra- red cartridges. When each of these cartridges fired, it sent out a very hot infra-red heat source in the form of a bright flare, just like a firework. They were, and still are used to confuse and deflect any heat seeking missiles fired at an aircraft by any belligerent. Such missiles are designed to home in on the hottest part of the aircraft, its engines. The infra-red flares burn at a much hotter temperature than the engines and thus the missiles chase the flares instead of the aircraft. You, the reader, might have seen these flares in action on television news broadcasts or in films where military aircraft trail several, what look like, pretty lights or fireworks.

AND FINALLY...

Back in the day...

A Big Mac was something you wore when it was raining.

A takeaway was a mathematical problem.

Twitter was the noise a bird made.

A microwave was a ripple on the sea.

A mobile phone had a long lead which led to a wall socket.

Pot was something you kept under the bed.

Drugs were headache tablets.

Suitcases did not have wheels.

Curry was a surname.

'Getting High' was when you approached the top of a mountain.

Only poor people had wooden floors.

Internet was where you put a fish after catching it.

Rebooting was when you bought a new pair of shoes.

Lunch was dinner and dinner was supper.

A laptop was the top of your thighs.

A tablet was something you got from the chemist.

Throwing snowballs and playing conkers were harmless.

e-bay was what a Geordie called a beach.

The only choice with crisps was whether or not to put the salt in.

Water came out of a tap and not from a bottle.

Frozen foods were called lollipops.

Software was clothes made from wool.

A freezer was a really cold day.

Eating raw fish was called poverty; not Sushi.

Sugar cubes were regarded as posh.

Fish didn't have fingers.

Indian restaurants were only found in India.

Healthy food was anything that was edible.

People ate their meals at tables where elbows were banned.

Amazon was a river in South America and had nothing to do with brown cardboard boxes and packaging.

Multiplication was known as 'Times Tables.'

One had to actually win something in order to get a trophy.

Paper bags were blamed for the destruction of trees – and plastic bags were considered the solution.

One didn't need an 'elf on the shelf' to motivate one to behave at Christmas – a 'stick on the shelf' kept one in line all year round.

THE END

IT REALLY *IS* THE END
THANK YOU FOR READING THESE STORIES.
I HOPE THAT YOU ENJOYED THEM

Lightning Source UK Ltd.
Milton Keynes UK
UKHW010646141022
410463UK00005B/286